Winner of the
British Columbia Genealogical Society's Family History Book Award

Winner of the
P.E.I. Museum and Heritage Foundation's Heritage Award

❊   ❊   ❊

"*The Bravest Canadian*, the story of Capt. Fritz Peters, is a tale that includes battlefield heroics, shadowy spies and political maneuvering that might well have been torn from a work of fiction. But the tale is real."

—*Oak Bay News*

"I enjoyed *The Bravest Canadian,* which tells the story of a remarkable Canadian Naval hero whose courageous exploits in both World Wars are, to date at least, largely unknown in Canada. In addition, the book provides a fascinating account of the life and incredible sacrifices of a Canadian family during a particularly interesting period of history."

—Vice Admiral (retired) Larry Murray
Grand President, Dominion Command
Royal Canadian Legion

"Thank you for sharing this wonderful, previously untold story."

—Kathy Wilson
President
New Brunswick Historical Society

"It is wonderful that this story has been made available for everyone to enjoy."

—CKNW, Vancouver

"His death-defying adventures sound like something out of a spy novel."

—Greg Nesteroff
Nelson Star

THE BRAVEST CANADIAN

THE BRAVEST CANADIAN

CANADIAN

Fritz Peters, VC
The Making of a Hero of Two World Wars

Sam McBride

GRANVILLE ISLAND
PUBLISHING

Library and Archives Canada Cataloguing in Publication

McBride, Sam, 1951-
   The bravest Canadian : Fritz Peters, VC : the making of a hero of two world wars / Sam McBride.

Includes bibliographical references and index.
ISBN 978-1-926991-10-8

   1. Peters, Fritz, 1889-1942—Correspondence. 2. World War, 1914-1918—Personal narratives, Canadian. 3. World War, 1939-1945—Personal narratives, Canadian. 4. Britain. Royal Navy—Officers—Correspondence. 5. Heroes—Prince Edward Island—Biography. I. Title.

D640.P44M33 2012   940.4'8171   C2012-902785-5

Editor: Kyle Hawke
Indexer: Bookmark: Editing & Indexing
Cover and Text Designer: Omar Gallegos

Granville Island Publishing Ltd.
212 – 1656 Duranleau St. Granville Island
Vancouver, BC, Canada V6H 3S4

604-688-0320 / 1-877-688-0320
info@granvilleislandpublishing.com
www.granvilleislandpublishing.com

First Published in 2012
Printed in Canada on recycled paper

Contents

Ancestry of Fritz Peters' father Frederick Peters

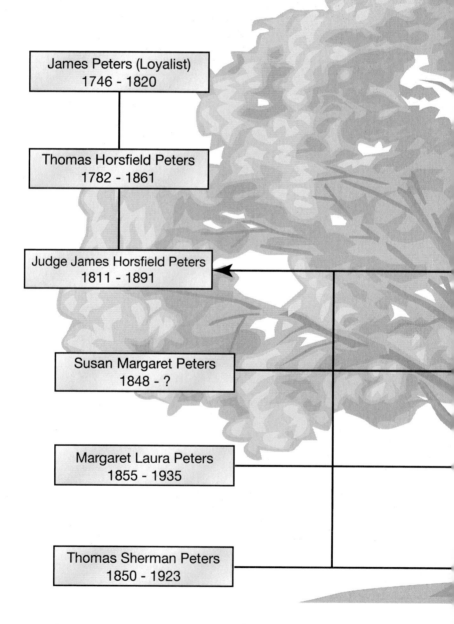

James Peters (Loyalist)
1746 - 1820

Thomas Horsfield Peters
1782 - 1861

Judge James Horsfield Peters
1811 - 1891

Susan Margaret Peters
1848 - ?

Margaret Laura Peters
1855 - 1935

Thomas Sherman Peters
1850 - 1923

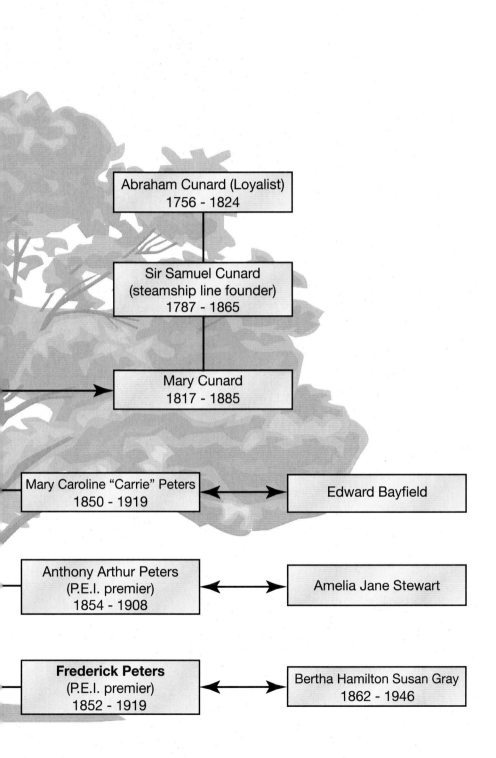

Abraham Cunard (Loyalist)
1756 - 1824

Sir Samuel Cunard
(steamship line founder)
1787 - 1865

Mary Cunard
1817 - 1885

Mary Caroline "Carrie" Peters
1850 - 1919

Edward Bayfield

Anthony Arthur Peters
(P.E.I. premier)
1854 - 1908

Amelia Jane Stewart

Frederick Peters
(P.E.I. premier)
1852 - 1919

Bertha Hamilton Susan Gray
1862 - 1946

Ancestry of Fritz Peters' mother Bertha Hamilton Susan Gray

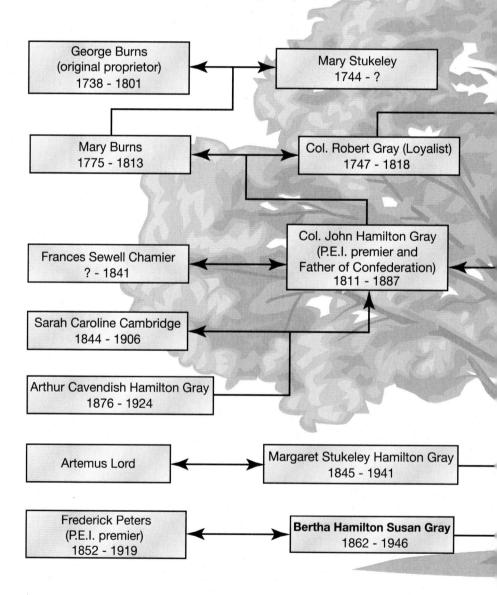

George Burns
(original proprietor)
1738 - 1801

Mary Stukeley
1744 - ?

Mary Burns
1775 - 1813

Col. Robert Gray (Loyalist)
1747 - 1818

Frances Sewell Chamier
? - 1841

Col. John Hamilton Gray
(P.E.I. premier and
Father of Confederation)
1811 - 1887

Sarah Caroline Cambridge
1844 - 1906

Arthur Cavendish Hamilton Gray
1876 - 1924

Artemus Lord

Margaret Stukeley Hamilton Gray
1845 - 1941

Frederick Peters
(P.E.I. premier)
1852 - 1919

Bertha Hamilton Susan Gray
1862 - 1946

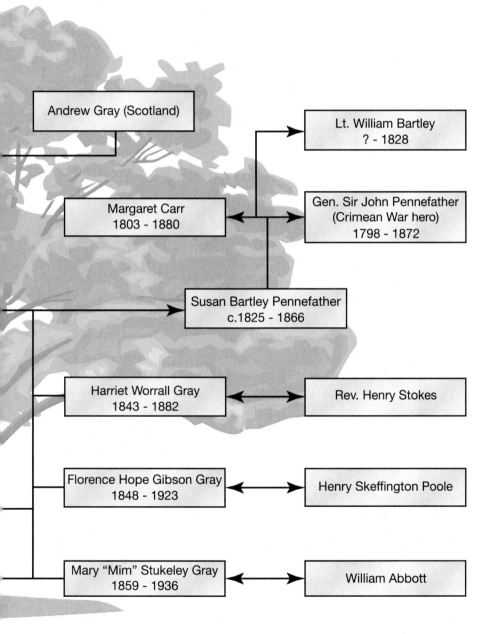

Andrew Gray (Scotland)

Lt. William Bartley
? - 1828

Margaret Carr
1803 - 1880

Gen. Sir John Pennefather
(Crimean War hero)
1798 - 1872

Susan Bartley Pennefather
c.1825 - 1866

Harriet Worrall Gray
1843 - 1882

Rev. Henry Stokes

Florence Hope Gibson Gray
1848 - 1923

Henry Skeffington Poole

Mary "Mim" Stukeley Gray
1859 - 1936

William Abbott

Children of Fred Peters and Bertha Gray

Frederick Peters
(P.E.I. premier)
1852 - 1919

John Francklyn Peters
1892 - 1915
Clerk, Bank of Montreal;
Pte., 7th B.C. Battalion

Gerald Hamilton Peters
1894 - 1916
Clerk, Union Bank;
Lieut., 7th B.C. Battalion

Noel Quintan Peters
1894 - 1964
Pte.,
Canadian Forestry Corps

Maxine Forbes-Roberts
1924 - 2010

John Archibald Fingland
1907 - 1997

Maj. Leigh Morgan McBride
1917 - 1995

Capt. Frederic Thornton Peters
VC, DSO, DSC and bar, DSC (U.S.), RN
1889 - 1942
Naval officer and spy school commander

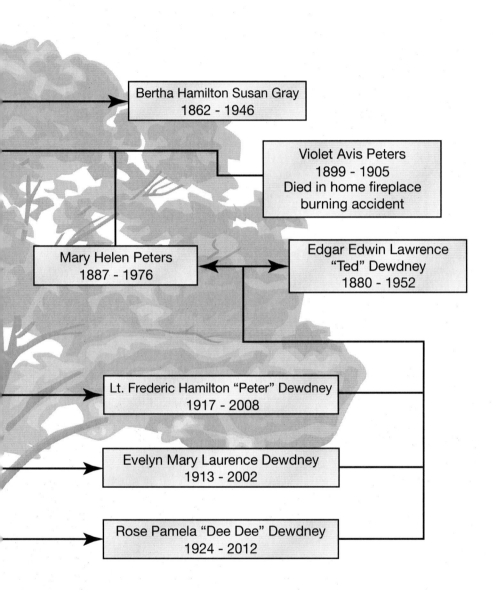

Bertha Hamilton Susan Gray
1862 - 1946

Violet Avis Peters
1899 - 1905
Died in home fireplace
burning accident

Mary Helen Peters
1887 - 1976

Edgar Edwin Lawrence
"Ted" Dewdney
1880 - 1952

Lt. Frederic Hamilton "Peter" Dewdney
1917 - 2008

Evelyn Mary Laurence Dewdney
1913 - 2002

Rose Pamela "Dee Dee" Dewdney
1924 - 2012

Acknowledgements

My maternal grandmother, Helen Peters Dewdney, lived in our house when I was growing up in Nelson, British Columbia, and was like a second mother to me. She often talked fondly of her little brother Fritz — always referring to him by that nickname, never by his given name Frederic. They were close siblings, just two years apart, and the two eldest of six children. She had a serene, supportive personality and was as much a peacemaker and diplomat as Fritz Peters was a warrior and hero. Like Fritz, she enjoyed intelligent conversation and was keenly aware of the world around her, including current events and politics.

Helen's personal papers included a large file of letters from her siblings to her mother Bertha that she inherited and kept safely stored in an antique suitcase. Before her death in 1976, Helen left a note with the material saying, "These can be burned, but they should be read first." When I discovered the file of letters a couple of years ago, I decided to transcribe them to share with my relatives. I soon realized the letters told lively stories about the Peters and Gray families, including dozens of letters from and about Fritz Peters that have never come to public view. They helped complete the story of her war hero brother Fritz, whose antiquated ideals, reclusive nature and exotic, unreported life story have stymied other biographical attempts. My first thanks must go to Bertha, Helen and my mother for resisting the temptation to toss — or burn — this material in their spring cleaning. In addition to the letters and photographs, a substantial portion of the Peters family's furniture, paintings and books have stayed in the family to this day.

I have been aided and encouraged in my research by three distant cousins: Dr. David Peters of St. John's, Newfoundland, Hugh 'Pete' Paton of Charlottetown, P.E.I., and the late Kim Abbott of Fallbrook, Ontario, all keenly interested in the life and story of Fritz Peters. I also appreciate the assistance of researcher William Glen in Prince Edward Island, Bob O'Hara and staff in England, who researched at the British National Archives at Kew, the staff of the provincial archives of Prince Edward Island and British Columbia, as well as those of the National Archives of Canada, numerous libraries, genealogical societies and Veterans Affairs Canada. Staff and volunteers at the modern-day successors to the schools Fritz attended — Bedford School and St. Piran's School (formerly Cordwalles) in England, and St. Michael's University School in Victoria — have been helpful in going through their archives. The interest and assistance of English writer Stephen Snelling, author of *VCs of the First World War: The Naval VCs*, who contacted the family in the 1990s with inquiries about Capt. Peters and has extensively researched the Oran harbour attack, is much appreciated.

Internet searches using names from the letters have often resulted in noteworthy findings. I received a wide range of information and support from participants in internet forums, particularly the World Naval Ships Forum and the Victoria Cross Forum. Through such forums and e-mail, I have contacted people all over the world with interest and insight into the Fritz Peters story, including Col. Brooke Thorpe in Australia, son of the Sunderland flying boat pilot who valiantly came to aid Fritz in Plymouth Sound in 1942, and Pete Mitchell, who assisted with the recovery of parts of a downed flying boat in the 1980s.

Special thanks go to Margaret Wanke for editing assistance, Sylvia Crooks for a thorough review and suggestions and Pamela McSwain for research at the Imperial War Museum and with *The Victor* comics. The professional assistance of Jo Blackmore, Kyle Hawke and Alisha Whitley at Granville Island Publishing is much appreciated.

While it is almost 70 years since Capt. Peters' heroism in Oran Bay in November 1942, many mysteries associated with his life remain. The Fritz Peters story is far from over. I am hopeful that publicizing names and details in his letters will result in new information emerging in the years ahead.

Sam McBride
Trail, British Columbia, Canada. 2011

INTRODUCTION

Death is nothing compared to dishonour.

— Frederic Thornton Peters, 1917

Despite winning a raft of medals for valour through two world wars, Capt. Frederic Thornton 'Fritz' Peters is relatively unknown among the 94 Canadian recipients of the Victoria Cross, or VC. This is partly because he spent little of his adult life in Canada. He was usually either at sea with the Royal Navy, on assignment with the SIS, the British Secret Intelligence Service, doing odd jobs in Gold Coast colony or England, or enjoying reunions with longtime navy buddies.

Some of Capt. Peters' military files were intentionally destroyed, probably because of his work between Royal Navy ship assignments with Britain's naval intelligence and the SIS. Normally, the awarding of a VC is cause for national celebration, but British authorities chose to downplay Peters' VC award because his heroism in the harbour of Oran, Algeria, against French defenders in 1942 was a sore point in relations between France and Britain when many French resumed as allies against the Nazis later in the war.

Of 181 VC recipients in the Second World War, he was the oldest at 53. Twenty-nine years earlier, he was the first Canadian to win the DSO, the British Distinguished Service Order medal, second only to the VC for British gallantry in battle, for saving the lives of men on HMS *Meteor* in the first battle of the First World War between the British and German fleets in the North Sea.

Fritz Peters' letters show he was a Victorian Age romantic with strong opinions on propriety and completely committed to old-fashioned personal standards of honour and duty. Restless by nature, he was easily bored and never settled for long in one place. Like his parents, he spent more than he earned and was burdened by debts throughout his life. While he fervently believed in the greatness of the British Empire, he was also a proud Canadian who for a time planned to run for political office in British Columbia.

Capt. Peters is rightly claimed as a native son by Prince Edward Island, where he was born and spent his early years. He was a direct descendant of one of the island's original proprietors — the first owners of property granted under British control — so his roots go back to the island's origins as a British colony. His later childhood was spent a continent away in Victoria, B.C., where he lived from age eight until enlisting in the Royal Navy at 15, aside from time at private schools in England. He grew up with a feel for both the Atlantic and Pacific oceans, which he came to know intimately as a man of the sea in the years ahead.

In keeping with his United Empire Loyalist roots, Fritz Peters had a pronounced dislike of the United States of America. He once said it was his eternal dread that someday Canadians would be indistinguishable from Americans. He grew up in an era when America was still officially Canada's enemy, and the Royal Navy base near his home on Vancouver Island was a check against American expansion. Fritz particularly disliked American brashness, self-centredness and fixation on money — traits also held, in his mind, by many Western Canadians.

Not surprisingly, sparks flew in the fall of 1942 when he had to work closely with equally prejudiced Americans in planning and carrying out the single most dangerous mission in the Allied invasion of North Africa. Decisions for the Oran harbour attack were made hastily and in an antagonistic atmosphere of mutual disrespect between British and American military planners and leaders. As commander of the mission, Fritz was in the thick of the hostile arguing back and forth. The bickering resulted in compromises which left each side unsatisfied.

While there was disagreement about tactics, Fritz's gallantry during the battle in the harbour drew universal acclaim. A mission leader of his age and rank would normally not be in the attack, but he insisted on participating once he knew the danger level. Through close to two hours of fighting — much of it at point-blank range — he astounded comrade and foe alike with his remarkable courage and skill in breaking through the harbour's protective barrier and forcing his ship near its target destination a mile and a half within a narrow, heavily-defended harbour.

The title of this book is an abbreviated form of the headline of an article about Fritz Peters in the 1991 *Starshell* publication of the Naval Officers Association of Canada titled "The Bravest Canadian of Them All". Depending on how different medals are valued, he rates among the most decorated Canadians in all services, and at the top of navy award-winners. He is alone among Canadians in winning multiple medals for valour in each of the world wars. Commander (Ret.) John Blatherwick, author of the *Canadian Medal Reference Book*, evaluated the achievements of the greatest Canadian heroes in an article titled "Who is the Bravest?". Blatherwick concluded, "I propose the bravest Canadian may well have been Frederic Thornton Peters, RN."[1]

His mother, out of touch with her son for decades, learned in correspondence with several of his friends and colleagues after his demise that Fritz was renowned for his lovable eccentricities and zest for life as much as for his heroism. Paymaster-Commander Sydney W. 'Swain' Saxton, RN, described him as "a typical Elizabethan gentleman adventurer" and the only navy man he ever knew who sharpened his sword before going into battle.[2] Commander David Joel, RN, said Fritz was "one of those rare romantic adventurers — 'Pirates' you might call them. . . completely without fear, dedicated to duty or their own interpretation of it, and tough as old rope."[3]

Describing Fritz in 1943, American war correspondent Leo 'Bill' Disher — survivor of the events at Oran and aboard HMS *Walney* — wrote, "His courage was massive, like his shoulders. In appearance he was strikingly calm, almost annoyingly so."[4]

Supreme Allied commander, U.S. General (and future President) Dwight Eisenhower was an admirer of Fritz, as was Winston Churchill, who approved his DSO in 1915 as First Lord of the Admiralty and personally briefed him before the Oran mission.[5] Churchill has often been quoted (without specific date or circumstance) as saying the attack through the boom of Oran harbour was the greatest, or most spectacular, British naval engagement since the Battle of Trafalgar in 1805.

Fritz had his share of detractors too, particularly American officers who blamed their heavy casualties in Oran harbour on his stubborn determination to carry out the mission in the face of fierce French fire. To this day, some descendants of American soldiers and marines who died in Oran harbour blame Capt. Peters for their deaths because he proceeded with a hazardous mission when he could have chosen to turn back to sea or to surrender.

Fritz was the type of man other men told stories about in bars, amazed by his ability to remain cool and calm in the heat of battle. As a lifelong bachelor with steadfast values, he was often picked as godfather to the sons of friends and relations.

Some who never knew him assumed he went out of his way to win medals in a quest for glory, but he was in fact a quiet hero who abhorred self-promotion, preferred to keep a low profile, avoided journalists like the plague and was cavalier with his medals, preferring not to wear them in public. Common refrains among his friends were, "Where's Peters?" and, "Whatever happened to Peters?"

The story of Peters' life is roughly two-thirds biography and one-third mystery. The biggest mystery is why he proceeded with the Oran mission even when it was crystal clear that powerful French shore batteries and warships were fully resisting the audacious attempt to take over the harbour. We can speculate on his reasons, but can never know for sure because a tragic air crash prevented his report on the mission from ever reaching Prime Minister Winston Churchill. More mystery revolves around his secretive life and puzzling whereabouts in the two decades between the world wars.

The heart of this book is the collection of 28 letters that he wrote and mailed to his family, mostly in the First World War period or shortly after, as well as one from the spring of 1942. He said he disliked writing, but in fact he was a good writer with interesting thoughts and a wry sense of humour. The letters included in this book are not edited for spelling or grammar, to allow the author's personality to show through.

Also referenced are letters from others about him, family notes, photographs and newspaper clippings in the Peters Family Papers that were securely kept for generations, first by Fritz's mother Bertha Gray Peters, then by his sister Helen Dewdney, and most recently by his niece Dee Dee McBride.

Detailed in Appendix A, Fritz Peters' roots give insight as to the origins of his fighting spirit, fondness for the sea, dedication to the British Empire and his old-fashioned personal code of honour. His letters reveal much about his character and motivations, and letters from others about him and his family, in Appendix B, help fill in gaps in what is known of his extraordinary life.

Chapter One

Great Expectations

My strength is as the strength of ten,
Because my heart is pure...

— "Sir Galahad" by
Lord Alfred Tennyson

Imagine the scene.

You are a middle-aged Canadian serving in the British Royal Navy in charge of a mostly American task force. You're commanding an extremely hazardous mission against well-armed French defenders who were once steadfast allies but are now under the thumb of Nazi conquerors. You received confusing orders from the commander of the Allied campaign to capture Oran, the swaggering Gen. Fredendall, who would later be exposed as one of the worst field commanders in U.S. Army history.

Your ship, HMS *Walney,* has successfully broken into the harbour in the dark of night but is now smack in the middle of a congested Algerian port, taking hit after hit from shore guns and French warships, some of them just yards away.

Most of the crew is either dead, seriously injured or blown into the water, so you have to fearlessly scramble from one end of the ship to the other to get landing lines in place so you can take over the largest French warship with a commando force. *Walney* and her sister ship *Hartland* are on fire, ammunition and depth charges are exploding, casualties are horrific, but somehow you manage to remain calm and collected, determined to somehow take control of the harbour so it can be used immediately for the massive Allied invasion of French North Africa. No one who witnesses the hellish scene will ever forget it. The famed *The Charge of the Light Brigade* in the Tennyson poem you memorized as a boy, was a picnic in comparison.

Ironically, one of the greatest movies in history, *Casablanca*, set in the French colony of Morocco after Germany conquered France, finishes production in November 1942, just as Allied troops are landing on beaches in Algeria and Morocco. The Allies have to deal with unpredictability, intrigue and conflicting loyalties similar to the setting of the fictional story in the movie. Unfortunately, the French commander at Oran harbour does not convert to the Allied side when it really counts, like Captain Louis Renault's last-minute conversion in the movie.

You wonder what happened to the coup by pro-Allied French officers that was supposed to happen in concert with the invasion. You'll try anything to achieve the mission's objectives, but you'll never lower the Royal Navy's White Ensign or the U.S. Stars and Stripes flag in surrender.

* * *

How did Frederic Thornton 'Fritz' Peters find himself in this unimaginable situation? The story begins with his parents, Frederick Peters and Bertha Gray, both born and raised in peaceful Prince Edward Island, in prominent families of Canada's Atlantic coast establishment.

Several ancestors on both sides of the family were larger-than-life characters who dominated the political, business and military scene of their time. Significantly, three of Fritz's grandparents were direct descendants of United Empire Loyalists who stayed true to King George in the American Revolution. The fourth grandparent was the daughter of a prominent British general in the Anglo-Irish aristocracy. Common threads among them — enthusiastically inherited by Fritz — included reverence for the British Empire, antagonism towards the United States of America, knowledge of British history and enjoyment of Victorian-era novels, music and poetry.

WAR HEROES AND A FATHER OF CONFEDERATION

Fritz's mother, Bertha, was the youngest daughter of Col. John Hamilton Gray, a household name in P.E.I. owing to his role as host and chairman of the historic Charlottetown Conference in 1864. Premier of the Island colony between 1863 and 1865, Gray was a vigorous supporter of British colonies north of the United States joining together in a new, self-governing nation. Though his time in politics was brief, he is remembered in history among the esteemed group of men who created Canada, known as the Fathers of Confederation.

At two years of age, Bertha was too young to remember the occasion, but later in life she often heard stories from her sisters of the night the family home, known as Inkerman House, was filled with Charlottetown Conference delegates. On Saturday, September 3, 1864, delegates had dinner on the ship *Queen Victoria* after their third day of meetings. Then Gray invited everyone to an after-dinner party at Inkerman House. Bertha and her four-year-old sister Mary were introduced to the gathering, and their teenaged sisters Margaret and Florence helped with the hosting. The story in the family was that enthusiasm for Confederation increased that night in relation to the amount of liquor consumed.

Col. John Hamilton Gray was a career officer in the British Army, serving primarily with the Dragoon Guards. His military career coincided with an era of peace in Europe, but he had plenty of stories to tell his children of skirmishes with rebellious forces in the far reaches of the British Empire, including an episode in South Africa in the mid-1840s where he led a charge to destroy an enemy gun emplacement.[1] According to his daughter Florence, who served as the family historian, the action would have qualified for the Victoria Cross, but this was a decade before Queen Victoria established the medal in 1856 to honour British heroes from the Crimean War and subsequent action.

Gray's father, Scotland-born Col. Robert Gray of Virginia, was a leader among Loyalists in battles against the colonial rebels in the American Revolutionary War. He helped form a regiment loyal to King George III and was in the thick of heavy fighting for several years. The land grants and appointments he gained in P.E.I., in appreciation of his loyalty and service, were the basis for the Gray family's prominence in Charlottetown in the 19th century.[2]

John Hamilton Gray idolized his father-in-law, Gen. Sir John Lysaght Pennefather, who defeated a much larger force of Russians in heavy fog in the Battle of Inkerman in the Crimean War. Gray expressed his admiration for Pennefather by naming his new Charlottetown estate Inkerman House, and by landscaping the trees on the road approaching the estate to represent the order of battle in Pennefather's famous victory.[3]

When Fritz Peters was a boy, much of the dinner table discussion and bedtime stories centred on the military exploits of the two Cols. Gray and Gen. Pennefather, each of whom was "grievously wounded" at least once in their military career, according to family history notes compiled by Bertha's sister Florence Gray Poole. Not surprisingly, the Pennefather and Gray fervour for military service continued with the Peters children, particularly Fritz.

BERTHA READ VORACIOUSLY

Bertha was in an unusual family situation because she was 19 years younger than her eldest sister Harriet and 18 years older than her youngest step-brother, Hamilton E. J. Gray. After her mother's death in 1866 when Bertha was four, her father remarried. Bertha was in her teens when her

Bertha Gray Peters, mother

stepsister, Rose and stepbrothers Arthur and Hamilton were born. Only Arthur lived to adulthood. Harriet was out of the house before Bertha was born, as she was sent by her parents to live with, and care for, her aging Pennefather grandparents in England.

Bertha was educated at home by tutors as well as regular lessons she and Mary received from much-older sisters Margaret and Florence. She inherited the Gray appetite for books, reading everything she could get her hands on, including dictionaries and encyclopedias. Many years later, her grandchildren were amazed by her depth of knowledge of the world and her brilliance in playing word games and solving puzzles. She took great pride in her ancestry and enjoyed describing herself to new acquaintances as a Daughter of Confederation.

She was a woman of fierce will and strongly-held opinions. Though more Scottish than English in her roots, Bertha was an ardent anglophile who took advantage of every opportunity to travel to England. In her mind, London — with its palaces, museums and connections to history and political power — was the Centre of the Universe. The flip side of her love of England and everything English was disapproval of the United States of America, in her mind the ungrateful former colony that turned its back on the British Empire.

STEAMSHIPS AND POLITICS

Fritz's father Frederick Peters did not take a back seat to his wife in telling of great men in his family tree.

Frederick was a grandson of Sir Samuel Cunard, one of the greatest businessmen in Canadian history. Mobility between Europe and North America increased tremendously in the mid-19th century as a result of steam-driven passenger service pioneered by Cunard, and he had a large role in the economic development of the Maritime provinces.[4] He was also a strong family man who cherished his nine children and dozens of grandchildren. His eldest daughter Mary Cunard married James Horsfield Peters and their children included Fritz's father Frederick Peters. As a boy,

Frederick got to know his grandfather Samuel well from Cunard's regular trips to Charlottetown to visit his daughter Mary and her husband, who was Cunard's lawyer and agent for P.E.I. interests before his appointment as judge in 1848.

Cunard won and lost fortunes several times in his business career, in the end leaving a substantial inheritance to each of his children. He encouraged grandson Frederick Peters to aspire to greatness and not be afraid to take risks. The Cunard Steamship Lines heritage was likely a factor in Samuel Cunard's great-grandson Fritz's affection for ships and the sea.

Samuel's father, Pennsylvania shipbuilder Abraham Cunard, was a Loyalist, as was Judge Peters' grandfather James Peters of New York, who settled in New Brunswick and established a tradition in the Peters family of lawyers, judges and politicians. So it was no surprise when Frederick Peters became a lawyer and entered politics.

FATHER FREDERICK BECOMES PREMIER IN 1891

Like many lawyers, Fritz's father Frederick Peters looked to involvement in politics and government as a way to serve his province while at the same time advance his livelihood and career. He first won a seat in the Prince Edward Island legislature in January 1890 when Fritz was still a baby. Within a year, Frederick was leader of the Liberal party and on April 21, 1891, he began as the province's first Liberal Premier and Attorney General. As Premier, Frederick Peters is best remembered for enacting legislation that amalgamated the two-house legislature into a single legislature, in line with other provinces.

Frederick Peters, father

Federally, Frederick Peters was a longtime ally of Liberal leader

Sir Wilfrid Laurier. Many years later, his daughter Helen Dewdney would recall chanting "Up with Sir Wilfrid, Down with Sir John!" in the 1891 federal election campaign, referring to Laurier and the Conservative Prime Minister Sir John A. Macdonald. Helen and other children were coached to sing the first part of the chant in a bright, cheery voice, then the latter phrase in a low, disdainful tone.[5]

In that era, a premier's salary was modest — just $1,000 per year[6] — so Frederick Peters often performed legal work on the side. A major project involved serving as counsel for the British/Canadian side in the Bering Sea Sealing Dispute, where he worked closely with federal Conservative Marine and Fisheries Minister Charles Hibbert Tupper of Halifax. Tupper was the son of the Nova Scotia Premier and Father of Confederation Sir Charles Tupper who served briefly as Prime Minister of Canada in 1896 and was well-known to the Peters and Gray families from more than three decades of Maritime politics.

Americans laid claim to all seal harvesting in the Bering Sea based on their purchase of Alaska from the Russians, but this was disputed by Britain, Canada and other countries. The August 1893 decision of an international arbitration panel solidly in favour of Britain's position was a feather in the cap for Peters and Tupper. The latter was knighted for his efforts, but not Frederick Peters, perhaps because of his prominence in the Liberal party, which was out of power.

While in Victoria, British Columbia, for meetings on the sealing dispute, Peters and Tupper were greatly impressed by the city's scenic beauty and mild weather, vowing to move there someday with their families. They expected the B.C. economy to grow as a result of the recent completion of the Canadian Pacific Railway across the country.

As leaders in their profession, the two men were among the organizers of the inaugural meeting of the Canadian Bar Association in Montreal in September 1896. Attendees at the conference included Tupper's Halifax law partner, Robert Borden, a future Prime Minister of Canada. The gathering elected Fred Peters as a vice-president of the new association, and Tupper as a member of the governing council.[7]

WESTWARD WITH THE GOLD RUSH

The Tupper-Peters plan to move across the continent and establish a law practice in Victoria was expedited by the spectacular news, in the spring of 1897, of discovery of gold in Klondike Creek, near Dawson City in the Yukon, the previous summer. Like millions around the world, the two Maritimers wanted to get in on the prosperity of the gold rush in some way. They saw that the city of Victoria stood to gain as a supply point for

The three Peters children shortly after birth of baby Jack Peters in 1892. Five-year-old Helen is at left, and at right is three-year-old Fritz Peters in a sailor suit.

people and goods going to and from the Klondike. Frederick's bombshell announcement that he was resigning as Premier as of October 27, 1897, to move west was a shock to his cabinet, caucus and other Islanders. Nevertheless, there were many well-wishers at his farewell party.

As leader of the government, Frederick Peters knew better than anyone that the island's economy had stalled, population was declining and prospects for future prosperity in a nation focused on the West were bleak. P.E.I. historian Andrew Robb described the political culture of the island at the time as "boisterous, parochial and permeated by patronage and petty corruption".[8] Fred had had enough of political life and vowed to never get involved in politics again. In retrospect, the family did not let the island down, as four years later Frederick's younger brother Arthur Peters — also a Liberal lawyer — took over as both P.E.I. Premier and Attorney General, serving seven years until his death in office in 1908.

The news that two leading lights of the Maritime legal and political scene were moving to Victoria was greeted triumphantly by West Coast newspapers. The duo was regarded as a "tough team to beat" [9] because of their capabilities and connections to both national parties. Brimming with confidence, Tupper and Peters bought land in the new Oak Bay community east of Victoria, developed by architect Francis Rattenbury, designer of the provincial legislature buildings and other B.C. landmarks.

Impressive, complementary seafront bungalows designed by the Rattenbury firm were built on adjoining lots in 1898 for the Tupper and Peters families. An early business partner of the duo in Victoria was the Hon. Edgar Dewdney, the pioneer B.C. trail-builder and former federal cabinet minister in Conservative governments, who had recently completed a term as B.C.'s Lieutenant-Governor. Dewdney was uncle and guardian of 17-year-old Edgar Edwin Lawrence 'Ted' Dewdney, who was beginning a long career with the Bank of Montreal, and would later marry Fritz's sister Helen.

MINING INVESTMENTS TANK

Buoyed by the optimism and enthusiasm of the Gold Rush, Frederick Peters invested heavily in mining ventures, which faded away as the stampeders left the Yukon for new gold finds in Alaska. This was the start of money problems that would dog him and his family for the rest of his life. It was particularly painful for someone who had grown up in a well-off family and whose wife expected to continue living in the style to which she had become accustomed, including the best private schooling in England for the children.

Tupper and Peters could not work as lawyers immediately after arriving in B.C. because regulations required six months of residency. This was the first of many frustrations Frederick would encounter in his new life on the West Coast. With an eye to expansion and connection with the Gold Rush, the Tupper and Peters law firm established branch offices in Vancouver, New Westminster and Dawson City, but business was much less than they anticipated.

Frederick vowed to give up politics when he left P.E.I., but in 1900 he was so angry at B.C. Premier Joe Martin — who he described as a "rash, experimental man" — that he came out strongly against him, even though he was a fellow Liberal.[10]

STOPPED A ROBBERY

Frederick never served in the military, but he was recognized as a Good Samaritan hero on December 10, 1900, when he stopped a robbery in progress while in Vancouver on business. A robber was pointing a pistol at a man with his arms in the air, and was going through his pockets when Fred came by in a horse-drawn cab, seized the driver's whip and hit the robber with the butt end. The robber pointed his gun at Fred, but decided to run away rather than pull the trigger. The headline of the *Mail and Empire* news story was, "At Point of Revolver Hon. Fred Peters Distinguishes Himself and Intimidates a Robber".

PARTNERSHIP ENDS

By 1902, Frederick Peters and Sir Charles Hibbert Tupper had parted ways in their law firm. Peters continued to practice in economically stagnant Victoria. Tupper worked in rapidly-growing Vancouver.

The outcome of the Alaska Boundary Dispute in October 1903 was a huge disappointment for Canadians, especially for Frederick Peters, whose reputation suffered because of his involvement with the case as a researcher and his longtime association with Britain's arbitrator Lord Alverstone, who stunned Canadians by casting the deciding vote for the Americans. Frederick's link with Alverstone went back a quarter-century to his time as a law student in England training under Alverstone.[11] U.S. President Theodore Roosevelt had threatened to send in troops if the dispute had not gone his way. The bullying was one more reason for 14-year-old Fritz Peters to hold a lifelong grudge against Americans.

Chapter Two

Growing Up on Two Canadian Coasts

*It is upon the Navy under the Good Providence of God that
the safety, honour and welfare of this realm do chiefly depend.*

— King Charles II of England

Like his father, Fritz Peters was born in stately Sidmount House in
Charlottetown. He arrived September 17, 1889, as the first son of Fred
and Bertha and two-year-old Helen's little brother. Jack came three years
later and in 1894 Gerald and Noel arrived as fraternal twins. In 1899, after
the family moved to Victoria, B.C., daughter Violet was born.

In Charlottetown, Fritz attended St. Peter's Anglican Church School
and also learned from tutors, his parents and from reading on his own.
Like the rest of his strongly anglophile family, he enjoyed reading and
discussing English history and the novels of Charles Dickens, Sir Walter
Scott and William Makepeace Thackeray. They read and memorized the
poetry of Lord Alfred Tennyson, particularly his rousing tribute to British
heroism in battle, *The Charge of the Light Brigade*, about an ill-fated but heroic
cavalry charge in the Crimean War. The family also enjoyed Tennyson's
The Revenge: A Ballad of the Fleet, about the Elizabethan naval hero Sir
Richard Grenville whose flagship made a heroic stand against a fleet of
Spanish galleons to enable other English warships to escape from an ambush.
Like all British Empire enthusiasts, Peters family members were keen readers
of Rudyard Kipling, who celebrated the Empire in stories and poems.[1]

With Helen playing the piano, the family sang songs from Gilbert and
Sullivan operettas that gently criticized British institutions, including the
Royal Navy in HMS *Pinafore*. One of the memorable characters in *Pinafore*
was a First Lord of the Admiralty who gained his position by keeping
"close to his desk" and "never going to sea". This entertaining satire may
have contributed to Fritz's aversion to desk jobs in his career.

BROTHERS WERE ALL DIFFERENT

Each of the four Peters brothers was markedly different. The younger brothers looked up to Fritz as their leader, and to Helen as a second mother. Jack's letters show he was more of a regular, happy-go-lucky boy, content to let Fritz take the hero role. Gerald was the intellectual among the children, preferring to read poetry and watch plays rather than participate in marching and rifle practice. Noel was handicapped with a moderate — though noticeable — mental disability that made his life miserable in an era when there was little understanding of, or allowance for, such handicaps. There is no record of Noel being diagnosed or receiving medical assistance for the problem. Bertha felt no qualms in openly treating Gerald as her favourite child and Noel her least favourite. The children got used to her discrimination among them and, aside from Noel, it did not appear to bother them.[2]

Like his grandfather Col. John Hamilton Gray, Fritz was keen on soldiering from his earliest days. He played with toy soldiers, read of the great battles of history, and dreamed of one day being a soldier. It was his obsession with all things military that led his family to nickname him 'Fritz', alluding to the stereotype of a Prussian officer totally committed to military life.

The move all the way across Canada to Victoria on Vancouver Island in early 1898 was a dramatic change for the Peters family. They brought hundreds of books and numerous pieces of furniture they cherished from their Charlottetown home, including a dining room table from Inkerman House that Bertha inherited from her father. In the years ahead, Bertha and her descendants made a point of mentioning to visitors that "the Fathers of Confederation sat around that table".

STRONG CONNECTION WITH THE TUPPERS

After his retirement from politics at age 75, the Father of Confederation Sir Charles Tupper was a regular visitor to his son Sir Charles Hibbert Tupper's home in Oak Bay, where he often encountered Fritz and other Peters children, who spent much of their time next door playing with the Tupper children who were of similar age.

Eight-year-old Fritz's bent changed from army to navy as a result of watching the impressive warships of the Royal Navy, from the backyard of his Oak Bay home, as they steamed to and from the Navy's Pacific Station at Esquimalt, adjacent to Victoria. The Peters family regularly travelled to Esquimalt to visit Fred's cousin Col. James Peters, who was in charge of coastal defence as District Officer Commanding, British Columbia.

In addition to getting together with Col. Peters' family, the visits often included tours of warships in the harbour. In the previous decade, Col. Peters was in command of the battery that built the Work Point Barracks in Esquimalt, parts of which were still used for Canadian defence purposes more than a century later.[3] As the head army man of the Victoria region and a prominent pioneer of West Coast defence, he had a free hand in showing friends and relations around the naval base facilities and visiting warships moored in the harbour.

A key attraction of naval service for Fritz was the romance of the Navy as Britain's Senior Service — the force that enabled a small island to rule over an empire encompassing a quarter of the world's land area and population.

With its large base close by, the Royal Navy had a huge impact on society and culture in Victoria — to the point that the city on the southern tip of Vancouver Island was known for being "more English than England". In contrast, mainland British Columbia was more influenced by other Western Canada provinces and the United States.

CHARACTER-BUILDING AT BOLTON SCHOOL

In Victoria, Fritz attended a small private school operated by Reverend W.W. Bolton out of his home on Belcher Avenue.[4] At Cambridge University in England, Bolton was a champion runner and keen on rugby, football/soccer, long distance swimming and boxing — games and skills he emphasized at his school, in the English private school tradition. Bolton was known for implanting in all boys his values of gentlemanly conduct, good manners, sportsmanship and athletic ability.

At the Peters Oak Bay home in 1906 are, from left: mother Bertha, daughter Helen with dog, son Noel and son Gerald.

In 1908, Bolton joined Rupert V. Harvey, headmaster of a school in Vancouver, and another partner, to form University School.[5] Shortly before the First World War, Fritz met with Harvey to discuss the ideal characteristics of a schoolmaster, a profession Fritz was considering at the time.

Fritz at his first private school at Bedford, England, in about 1900.

20TH CENTURY BEGINS WITH PRIVATE SCHOOL AT BEDFORD, ENGLAND

Recognizing the limitations of Bolton's small school for Fritz, his parents enrolled him at Bedford Grammar School in England in 1900. Bertha's stepmother Sarah Caroline Gray had moved with her son Arthur to Bedford, north of London, after her husband John Hamilton Gray's death. Jack Peters began at the Bedford school with his brother Fritz and continued there for three years.[6] Records are not clear as to whether the boys boarded at the school or stayed with Sarah, but the latter is likely in light of the family's financial distress.

At the same time, sister Helen went to Bedford High School for Girls, later studying piano and music at the Royal Conservatory of Music in London. Helen often told her children and grandchildren of standing with her brothers on a London street in January 1901 watching Queen Victoria's funeral procession.

CORDWALLES PREPARATORY SCHOOL FOR FUTURE NAVY OFFICERS

After a year at Bedford, Fritz studied for three years at Cordwalles Boys School in Maidenhead, Berkshire, known for preparing boys for a career as naval officers. Cordwalles counted Benjamin Disraeli among its alumni, and had Navy 1 and Navy 2 courses in its curriculum. School records show that Fritz was a capable if not brilliant student and took on leadership roles in his dormitory. The *Cordwalles Chronicle* school magazine records Fritz as a prize-winner in the Navy 2 class in 1903. He was tied for first in his French class and fourth in mathematics.

He wasn't great at sports but was praised for his enthusiasm and for always giving his best effort. Fritz played on the 'second 11' of the school's cricket team and football team. As a cricketer, the magazine records him as "Very slow bat. Bowls a little. Keen cricketer." As a football forward, he was rated "Fast and dribbles well. Apt to fall down at critical moments."[7]

One of his classmates and cricket teammate at Cordwalles was Frederick Dalrymple-Hamilton, who would train with Fritz as a cadet, be a lifelong friend and rise to Rear Admiral with the Royal Navy.

Fritz, middle of top row, with sport teammates at Cordwalles School, about 1903.

CHAPTER THREE

1905
GOING TO SEA IN KING EDWARD'S NAVY

I must go down to the seas again, to the lonely sea and the sky,
And all I ask is a tall ship and a star to steer her by

— "Sea Fever"
by John Masefield

In January 1905 at age 15, Fritz commenced service with the Royal Navy. His parents hoped he would be stationed close to home at Esquimalt for a five-year term, as was common for cadets in the past. But the navy closed its Pacific Station in March 1905 because Britain was marshalling resources to home waters in response to the rising threat of Germany. Bertha later said Fritz would have joined the Royal Canadian Navy if it had existed at the time, but the *Naval Service Act* that created the RCN was five years in the future, so the only navy for a young Canadian was the prestigious Royal Navy — ruler of the sea and bulwark of the Empire.[1]

For a year and a half after enlistment, Fritz trained in and around England on HMS *Britannia* with other cadets, including Sydney W. 'Swain' Saxton and Cromwell Varley, who would serve as fellow naval officers in the First World War, be among Fritz's lifelong friends

Fritz in naval uniform, in about 1906.

16

and choose Fritz to be godfather of their sons. It was an exciting time to be in the navy, as the dynamic Admiral John A. 'Jackie' Fisher, in charge as First Sea Lord, replaced virtually all existing vessels with modern warships, most notably HMS *Dreadnought*, which made all other battleships in the world obsolete. Fisher also developed destroyers — compact, speedy and well-armed warships for protection against torpedo boats and submarines. It would be on destroyers, as an officer and later in command, that young Fritz Peters would make a name for himself in the First World War.

In 1906, Fritz went to sea as a midshipman in the Channel Fleet on HMS *Vengeance* under Admiral Arthur 'Tug' Wilson, who Fritz later described as "one of England's greatest admirals".[2] Wilson was known for his complete dedication to the navy — to the point that he never married, which may have influenced Fritz, also a lifelong bachelor. Wilson was also noted for his economy with words. After winning the Victoria Cross in 1884 for heroism in the Sudan, he wrote in his diary: "Docked ship. Received VC." Wilson's modesty regarding his medals may also have influenced Fritz, who preferred to downplay the medals and other honours he received.[3]

Royal Navy men beside wreckage of the Messina Earthquake, 1908, where Fritz won his first medal.

RESCUE WORK AT MESSINA EARTHQUAKE

Fritz was on the battleship HMS *Duncan,* wintering at Malta, when a 7.5 magnitude earthquake and tsunami hit Messina in northeast Sicily on December 28, 1908, killing about 70,000 Italians. He was part of a contingent of Royal Navy men who rushed to assist with rescue and relief operations. For leading shore rescue parties, Fritz received his first medal at 19, the Messina Silver Earthquake Medal, personally presented by Italy's King Victor Emmanuel.

In July 1909, Fritz was promoted to acting sub-lieutenant and commenced studies at Portsmouth and later at the Royal Naval College at Greenwich. From there he went to the Navy's China Station at Weihaiwei on the destroyer HMS *Otter* for gunboat duty protecting British commerce and serving as a check on the nearby German sphere of influence. His promotion to lieutenant came through in March 1912.

SERVICE AND SOCIETY AT THE CHINA STATION

Writing in the 1950s, Fritz's colleague Commander David 'Solly' Joel, RN, said that in his 27 years in the navy he never encountered so close a friendship as that which existed between the First Lieutenants of the China Destroyer Flotilla between 1910 and 1912. "Our ships were rivals in every way — smartness, games, boat races in the flotilla, regattas — but there was nothing but deep friendship between the Number Ones," he wrote in unpublished memoirs.[4] He said the most memorable Number Ones (second-in-command officers) were: future admiral and diplomat Cedric 'Hook' Holland, Harry Dunbar-Rivers, who served as a lieutenant in the First World War, and Fritz Peters. Fritz's nickname was Tramp — "for no reason at all", according to Joel.

Ironically, three decades later, Hook Holland and Fritz Peters would each have fateful encounters with obstinate French admirals in charge of ports at Oran in the French colony of Algeria: Holland at the military port of Mers-el-Kebir, on the west side of Oran Bay, in Britain's drastic action against French warships after Germany's conquest of France, and Fritz at Oran's nearby city harbour 28 months later in the Allied invasion of North Africa.

Weihaiwei port in Shandong province in northeast China, where Fritz was based, was an outpost of the British Empire with a lively social environment for the young naval officers, among other expatriates. Writing in the 1950s, Margaret 'Betty' Joel, daughter of Sir James Stewart Lockhart, Commissioner at Weihaiwei at the time, recalled the happy days of parties and dances with Fritz and other Navy men of the China Station:

"And so mad Peters has gone after all, another sweet and delightful link severing our youth from us. I wept for him silently and secretly . . . . Mad Peters of the Wei-Hai days of the black eyes and white teeth and aloof humour . . . . We remember that splendid gay youth in the sunshine; the delightful capers, the nonsense and the dancing. How grateful I am for all those sweet delicious memories peopled by such gallant ones." [5]

Betty married Commander David Joel in 1918. By the 1930s, she was internationally famous as a furniture designer and interior designer in the art deco style.

HIJINKS IN SINGAPORE

Fritz's longtime friend Paymaster-Commander Swain Saxton told of pranks he, Fritz and other young navy men got up to one night while docked in Singapore. In the wee hours of a raucous night, they commandeered rickshaws near the Raffles Hotel and raced them as chariots across the city, with Fritz brandishing his walking stick high in the air as a battle sword. One of their mock battles ended with Fritz somersaulting several times before landing in a pile of dust. Then, seeing a prostitute walk by, Fritz righteously delivered a sermon on morality to her. This led to a heated argument with a Sikh policeman, which continued until they reached their exit dock, where the navy men had a rowboat for returning to their ship. Saxton pulled the rowboat away just as Fritz was climbing on, causing him to fall into the sea. "In those days we were quite wild animals," Saxon said. [6]

At the same time Fritz was chasing pirates and a hit with the ladies at Empire socials in China, his friend from Cordwalles School and training on *Britannia*, Lt. 'Freddie' Dalrymple-Hamilton, RN, was based in Scotland and part of the upper class social set with the Bowes-Lyon family. [7] He played cricket with the Bowes-Lyon brothers and was an admirer of their sister Rose, who rejected his offer of marriage. However, he stayed close to the family, attending the wedding of Rose's younger sister Elizabeth and the future King George VI in 1923. He continued to be a friend of the future Queen and Queen Mother until his death in 1972. Having Dalrymple-Hamilton as a friend and supporter could only benefit Fritz in his years ahead in the navy.

TRAGEDY IN VICTORIA

The first of many tragedies to strike the Peters family was the death of Fritz's six-year-old sister Violet in an accident in the family's Oak Bay home in November 1905. Helen recalled years later that her little sister burned to death when her clothes caught on fire when she was too close to one of the fireplaces the large drafty house used for heating. *The Colonist* reported she died at St. Joseph's Hospital and the funeral was at Christchurch Cathedral.

BOLD MOVE TO PRINCE RUPERT

Facing financial difficulties, Fred moved the family from Oak Bay, in about 1908, to a more modest home in Esquimalt.

After losing money in mining investments and seeing his lawyer income decline, Fred decided in 1911 to move to the brand new town of Prince Rupert, a soon-to-be-developed port in northwest B.C. just south of the Alaska Panhandle. This was in line with his optimism regarding the north, going back to the Klondike Gold Rush. He felt that to earn the fortune he so desperately wanted and needed he had to get in on the ground floor of a new boom community. When the opportunity to hold the position of Prince Rupert's City Solicitor came his way, he enthusiastically accepted the challenge.

However, soon after his arrival in Prince Rupert at age 59, the Grand Trunk Railroad's plans to establish a major new Canadian port derailed. The biggest blow was the drowning of Charles Melville Hays, the powerful President of the Grand Trunk Railroad and champion of Prince Rupert port development, when *RMS Titanic* sank in April 1912.

Returning in July 1913 from a trip to England with the mayor of Prince Rupert to secure financing for the new port, Frederick Peters told the *Montreal Gazette* that he was still confident Prince Rupert would thrive as "the next Vancouver". However, he and the fledgling city would struggle with its financial woes every year for the rest of his life. He took on the higher position of City Clerk in 1916.

MARRIAGE OF HELEN PETERS AND TED DEWDNEY

A happy event for the Peters family in June 1912 was the wedding, at St. Paul's Anglican Church in Esquimalt, of Helen to Ted Dewdney. Fritz was at sea and missed the wedding, as did father Frederick Peters, who was tied up with a city financial emergency in Prince Rupert. Frederick asked his cousin Col. James Peters — recently retired after a distinguished 42-year military career — to give away the bride on his behalf. Wedding guests included Ted's 77-year-old uncle and former guardian, the Honourable Edgar Dewdney.

Ted and Helen moved to Vernon, in the Okanagan region of central B.C., where he worked as an accountant with the Bank of Montreal. Their first child, Eve Dewdney, born in December 1913, was often mentioned in letters home sent by Fritz and his brothers.

Perhaps inspired by their brother-in-law Ted, Jack Peters and Gerald Peters both worked as bank clerks before the war — Jack with the Bank of Montreal and Gerald with the Union Bank. With his disability, Noel faced great difficulty in landing a job.

Helen Dewdney with baby Eve, early 1914.

RESIGNATION FROM NAVY TO EARN MORE MONEY

In the summer of 1913, Fritz resigned from the British Navy, giving as his reason the need to "add to my family's coffers".[8] He tried working as a salesman and in other odd jobs, and eventually his navy experience helped him land a position as third officer with the Canadian Pacific Railway, in the mountainous British Columbia interior, where the company had a fleet of ships for lake cargo and passenger service that connected with rail lines.

CHAPTER FOUR

1914 – 1915
BRAVING DAMAGED BOILERS IN THE BATTLE OF DOGGER BANK

For it's Tommy this, an' Tommy that, an' "Chuck him out, the brute!"
But it's "Saviour of 'is country" when the guns begin to shoot.

— "Tommy" by
Rudyard Kipling

At the outbreak of the First World War, the Peters family found themselves in financial straits in remote and rainy Prince Rupert, B.C. It went without saying that Fritz would rejoin the Royal Navy and the three younger boys would enlist in the army and do their part for the British Empire in its time of greatest need. Each of the three younger boys had taken cadet training in Victoria and later in Prince Rupert with the Earl Grey's Own Rifles militia, which mostly involved marching and shooting practice. Had the war come a decade earlier, Helen's husband Ted would have been in the First Contingent. The son of a Crimean War cavalry veteran,[1] he was an active member of the Rocky Mountain Rangers militia in Rossland for seven years in his twenties. At age 34 in 1914, he was supporting a wife and child and past ideal military age, so he did not join his brothers-in-law in military service.

Fritz didn't wait for a declaration of war before catching a ride on a tramp steamer back to England to rejoin the Royal Navy. On August 22, 1914, he began service as First Lieutenant on HMS *Meteor*, a recently-launched destroyer with top speed of 35 knots (65 km/hr).

He would soon hear of a disturbing development back home in B.C., as brother Gerald was rejected for army service because he failed the physical examination when he tried to enlist in Prince Rupert. In the following letter, Fritz encourages Gerald to try again for enlistment after doing an exercise program Fritz ordered for him to increase his upper body strength. To make his points, Fritz refers to the cheerful, big-hearted Mark Tapley character from the Charles Dickens novel *Martin Chuzzlewit* and quotes from "The Children's Song" of *Puck of Pook's Hill* by Rudyard

Kipling, the famous writer of the Empire who enthusiastically supported the Great War in his lectures and articles. It is ironic that the Kipling family was going through the same experience as the Peters. Kipling's only son Jack failed his enlistment physical because of very poor eyesight. With his father's help, Jack Kipling was eventually accepted into the army.[2] Lieut. Jack Kipling died in September 1915 in the Battle of Loos.

FRITZ TO HIS BROTHER GERALD   SEPTEMBER 4, 1914

Dear Gerald,

I was very sorry to hear that you failed in your endeavour to volunteer on account of your chest measurement. I can imagine you must be feeling badly about it. But don't be downhearted. Life is full of these little things: follow the footsteps of Mark Tapley and you cannot go far wrong. I trust you have made this gentleman's acquaintance in Martin Chuzzlewit. Anyhow to fail in this particular point is but a small thing and one — in your case — that is easily remedied.

I have written to a physical culture man in England instructing him to send you a course of exercises. Now if you faithfully and diligently follow these out, you will find in two or three months or perhaps half that time an immeasurable improvement of your physical fitness in every respect. I may say that I once got some exercises for my own use, but never had the energy to use them. I wish now that I had. Now you have a great incentive before you, the incentive to make yourself fit to serve the country.

Study friend Rudyard Kipling: "Teach us to keep ourselves always controlled and cleanly night and day, that we may bring, if need arise, no maimed or worthless sacrifice."

Now follow my advice and go right into this thing with all your heart and all your guts. Put your mind on it. Keep it always before you. Think about it at night before you sleep. Don't let it be away from your waking thoughts. Do all these things and in six weeks you will pass any medical examiner in the world. But dig your heels in and go like the devil at it.

This war is going to be a long business. Time to start in a new recruit at one end and come out — if you are lucky — a trained man at the other. But above all, don't lose heart. It is not given to every man to be so fortunate as to fight for his country. As soon as you are fit, go to the depot and present yourself and no doubt they will take you on. I have squared with this man for these exercises which I expect will shortly follow this letter.

Cheer up, F.T.P.

P.S. . . . I expect to go to sea in ten days.

At 6 feet 1½ inches, Gerald was thin and gangly, and his expanded chest did not meet the standard. Gerald was sensitive, intellectual and, quite literally, a mama's boy who would never choose army service in normal times but felt compelled to do his part in the war emergency. Perhaps to avoid the same examiners who assessed him in B.C., Gerald traveled to Montreal for a second try at enlisting. This time, he passed and was admitted as a private to the Royal Victoria Rifles 24th Battalion.

In failing the medical exam in Prince Rupert, Gerald was in good company. At the outbreak of war, John MacGregor took a train from his residence in northern British Columbia to Prince Rupert to enlist in the army. Like Gerald, he was rejected on medical grounds by the Prince Rupert doctor. Undaunted, he travelled to Vancouver where he passed the physical and joined the 11th Canadian Mounted Rifles (CMR). Rising to sergeant, lieutenant and then captain, MacGregor won a Distinguished Conduct Medal at Vimy Ridge. This was followed in the next year and a half by a Military Cross, then the Victoria Cross for daring and leadership on September 29, 1918, and then a bar to his Military Cross. He tried to serve in combat again in the Second World War but was recognized as a VC recipient and put in command.[3] MacGregor's record puts him alongside Fritz Peters among the bravest and most decorated Canadians.

JACK PETERS JOINS CANADA'S FIRST CONTINGENT

Gerald's older brother Jack Peters was the same height as Gerald but physically robust. He had no difficulty passing the physical, joining the 7th B.C. Duke of Connaught's Battalion in Canada's First Contingent. Like Gerald, he would do his duty but preferred to leave the heroics to big brother Fritz. In early 1915, he wrote to his mother from training camp in England: "You needn't worry about me because I don't intend to put my head up above the trench to shoot the Germans. Me for where the earth is thickest and highest." As it turned out, keeping low in the trenches was impossible for Jack and other Canadian soldiers in the Second Battle of Ypres in April 1915 because heavier-than-air poisonous chlorine gas released by the Germans settled at the bottom of trenches, forcing soldiers to the surface where they were easy prey for enemy guns.

Gerald's fraternal twin Noel tried to enlist but was rejected because of his mental disability, which was not as bad as it seemed from his appearance, but enough at that point of the war to keep him out of service. At 19, he was of ideal age for entering the military, so there was intense pressure in the community and within the family for him to serve. The stress from this rejection and subsequent harassment and bullying led to Noel suffering a serious nervous breakdown in the spring of 1915.

HOSPITAL SHIP SUSPECTED OF SPYING FOR U-BOATS

Fritz and other officers on destroyer *Meteor* were soon in the news for boarding the German hospital ship *Ophelia* on October 17, 1914, after the Battle off Texel, an island north of Amsterdam, and forcing it to port in Yarmouth, England. Fritz testified in an affidavit that the surgeon of *Ophelia* responded suspiciously when asked to explain the ship's movements. Fritz concluded that *Ophelia* "was guilty of rendering unneutral service, either by transmission of intelligence in the interests of the enemy, or improperly carrying warlike stores".[4] For violating the rules for hospital ships in the Hague Convention, the ship was confiscated and converted for British use. The Germans used the incident as justification for attacking Allied hospital ships later in the war.

HERO OF BATTLE OF DOGGER BANK

Fritz received his first honours for valour in the Battle of Dogger Bank on January 24, 1915. German warships had been shelling the eastern coast of Britain, hoping to draw out British warships so they could be attacked by U-boats. The conflict led to a chase in the North Sea at Dogger Bank above Denmark, about halfway between Britain and Germany. It was the war's first significant battle between British and German fleets in the North Sea.

Meteor, under Capt. Meade, was setting up to torpedo the slow German cruiser *Blücher* when it was hit by the last round from the cruiser before sinking — an 8.2-inch shell that hit *Meteor*'s engine room. With incredible calm and coolness, Lt. Fritz Peters rushed to the engine room — a scary place of scalding water and boiler explosions when damaged in battle — and made it safe. With fire spreading and leaking oil in the engine room threatening to explode, he was credited with saving the lives of two ratings and perhaps many more on board if there had been an explosion or the boilers had burst.[5] Another report said that he also pushed an unexploded shell overboard.[6]

For these actions, Fritz was the first Canadian ever to receive the Distinguished Service Order, or DSO, medal, second in rank only to the Victoria Cross as a British honour for bravery in battle. It was the highest honour bestowed in the aftermath of the Dogger Bank conflict. He initially received a Mention in Dispatches for the heroism and then, in March, 1915, King George V presented him with the DSO medal. The family's pride in his gallantry is shown in the following letters from brothers Jack and Gerald.

Jack mentions the three relatives in England who had an open door for visits by members of the Peters family: Bertha's sister Florence Poole in Guildford, Fred's cousin Helen Jane Francklyn (daughter of Sarah Jane Cunard) in Bristol and Fred's cousin Col. Henry Edward Mellish (son of Margaret Ann Cunard), whose residence was the stately home known as Hodsock Priory in Nottinghamshire.

Jack Peters at about 18 in 1910.

The Boggs fellow Jack recalls from militia training was Lieut. Herbert Boggs, 22, of the 7th Battalion, son of Beaumont and Louise May Boggs of Victoria, B.C. He died February 26, 1915, in the Ypres Salient, the first British Columbia boy to die in the war. The Boggs lived next door on Fort Street to the family of Brigadier General Arthur W. Currie, who sent his neighbours the official letter of condolence on the death of their son.[7]

JACK PETERS TO HIS BROTHER GERALD   MARCH 11, 1915

France

Dear Gerald,

    . . . I suppose you are in England by now . . . . You want to visit Aunt Florence and Aunt Helen and the Hodsock bunch if you get leave. They'll treat you well. Only take my tip and just spend a day at each place, because they are rather boring after that time . . .

    . . . You remember Boggs who used to command the High School cadets. He was killed by a sniper a few weeks ago . . . Pretty hard luck so early in the war.

    I'm writing this letter in the actual firing trench. Shells whistle over me every minute and now and again a bullet hits the parapet above . . .

    I suppose you know about Fritz winning the DSO and being mentioned in dispatches. Won't Father and Mother be tickled to death! I dare say he is quite satisfied, but I should think that it certainly should help his promotion a lot . . .

Good bye, Old Man
Jack

Writing from Montreal, Gerald thinks his mother was on her way to England to be there while her boys served in the war, but her trip was postponed due to a serious nervous breakdown suffered by Gerald's twin brother Noel.

In line with his extremely close relationship with his mother, Gerald regularly used pet names for her and himself in correspondence with her.

GERALD TO HIS MOTHER BERTHA   EARLY 1915

    . . . How proud you must be about Fritz. I got your letter and Aunt Florence's on the same day telling me of it. You must almost want to go back to Prince Rupert to be able to tell everyone . . .

Your loving,
Zarig

Bertha Peters desperately wanted to be close to her boys as they served in the war, particularly her favourite child and soulmate Gerald, who was training with the 24th Royal Victorian regiment and expected to soon go overseas. She arranged to travel to England in March 1915 to be there when Gerald arrived. Jack was already in France with the 7th Battalion, having arrived in England in November 1914, and spending a rainy winter training on Salisbury Plain. He embarked for France in February 1915 and saw his first action in March at the Battle of Neuve Chapelle.

Bertha was furious that Noel's illness would cause her to miss her trip to England and lose out on non-refundable expenses. However, she was able to get to England in July 1915, thanks to money raised by her sons from their military pay. For the next 16 months, Bertha stayed with relations or in rented cottages and flats, mostly in southeast England close to where Gerald was stationed, so they could get together on his leaves.

BAPTISM OF FIRE IN SECOND BATTLE OF YPRES

In mid-April 1915, Jack's battalion and other Canadians were in minor trench action in the Ypres Salient in the Flanders region of Belgium. They found the battlefield was still a stinking mess from the First Battle of Ypres the previous fall.

The Second Battle of Ypres began shockingly on April 22, 1915, when the Germans released poison gas against Allied troops, for the first time on the Western Front. It came as a complete surprise to the Allied soldiers, though there had been several warnings from German prisoners and deserters, which went unheeded because Allied authorities could not imagine their foe taking such a dishonourable action, one that was forbidden by international treaties.

Wind carried the heavier-than-air chlorine gas directly into the trenches of French Colonial troops, who found it unbearable and ran away from their lines in panic, leaving four miles of the front undefended. It was said that the French Colonials — mostly Algerians — ran so fast from the gas that their feet didn't touch the ground. The Germans did not expect such dramatic impact from the gas and were not prepared with reserves to immediately follow up on the breakthrough with attacks to capture Ypres and the Channel ports, which would have been devastating for the British.

This gave Canadians on the right flank some time to take emergency action to fill the breach in the line. Through great bravery and with heavy casualties over the next two nights and days, the green Canadian troops were able to establish some control in new lines of defence. Then, on April 24th, the Germans launched a full-scale early morning attack with intense shelling and poison gas directly against Canadian troops northeast of Ypres, including Jack's battalion, which came to the battle line out of reserve. The Germans also used flame-throwers for the first time in the war.

In addition to dealing with the gas — which some Canadians famously endured by covering their mouth and nose with urine-soaked handkerchiefs — the Canadians had to make do with problematic Ross rifles, which performed so poorly in battlefield conditions that many Canadians replaced them with Lee Enfield rifles taken from dead British soldiers. The battalion suffered 80 percent casualties in the fierce battle, including a substantial group of soldiers captured at St. Julien, a small village northeast of Ypres, after it was surrounded by the Germans. One of the prisoners taken was machine gun officer Lieut. Edward Bellew of the 7th Battalion, who received the Victoria Cross after the war for holding off a stream of German soldiers attempting to take over his trench.[8]

DISAPPEARED INTO THIN AIR

It was in the thick of this fighting that Pte. Jack Peters disappeared and was never seen or heard from again. Family letters show that a combination of wishful thinking and rumour caused the Peters family to be one hundred percent certain that Jack was safe as a prisoner of war. Fred's cousin Helen Francklyn in Bristol said a friend in Switzerland told her Jack was in the Celle Lager prison camp in Hanover. Always looking to see the bright side of a situation, Gerald said this was good news because the Saxons were less antagonistic to the British than Prussians and Bavarians.

The Hanover prison camp information was recorded unofficially in Jack's army file, but 13 months later on May 29, 1916, Canadian authorities learned from the Red Cross that the P.O.W. in Hanover previously identified as Jack Peters was definitely someone else, so Jack was declared in Canadian Army records to have died "on or after April 24, 1915." He may have disappeared into thin air when vaporized by a direct hit of a heavy shell, or his body may have been among the many thousands that were callously treated by both sides, with no effort made to record identification before bodies were buried in mass graves or used as fill for battle-related construction.

STEEL NERVES REQUIRED FOR DARING RESCUES AT SEA

In November 1915, Fritz was appointed to command a destroyer for the first time. HMS *Greyhound*, a 30-knot destroyer built in 1900, was the first of a succession of four destroyers under his command in the next four years. The DSO he earned at Dogger Bank made him a celebrity among naval officers, and he developed a reputation for courage and skilled seamanship in rescues of sailors and merchantmen struggling in the water after their ships were sunk by subs. On several occasions, his destroyers were almost hit by torpedoes as subs lay in waiting to attack rescue ships after the initial sinkings.

After suffering serious damage in the Battle of Dogger Bank, *Meteor* was towed home to England, where it was repaired and later used as a minelayer. In his pre-war service in the Royal Navy's China Station, Fritz had been on the 30-knot destroyer HMS *Otter*, launched in 1896. He was keenly aware of the age of his ships because speed was critically important in confrontations at sea.

In the following letter, undated but believed to be at the end of 1915 based on the ships mentioned, Fritz was so convinced brother Jack was safe as a prisoner of war that the subject did not come up in correspondence with his father.

He mentions seeing Lieut. Reginald Hibbert Tupper, a son of his father's former law partner in Victoria. The two boys were friends at the turn of the century when they were next-door neighbours in Oak Bay. Reginald was seriously injured at the Second Battle of Ypres. Like many soldiers, he had to overcome an addiction to morphine in his recovery, due to crude medical treatment at the front. He went on to a distinguished career in Vancouver as a lawyer and leader of the bar association. His younger brother, Capt. Victor Gordon Tupper, died at Vimy Ridge in 1917.

FRITZ TO HIS FATHER FREDERICK   DECEMBER 1915

You will see that I have left the Meteor some four months now. This craft is the same class as the Otter whom you may remember I was in at China in 1911. I am in command, but it is an empty honour and I would a good deal rather be where I was. One is practically out of the running here and, if anything did happen, one would merely swell the casualty lists. I had hopes of going East, but apparently unjustified.

How is Mr. Clements? I want to write to him concerning this surveying business and how it is looking up these days.

I saw Reggie Tupper in a hospital last August. He had been badly wounded and was then on the road to recovery but I should not think he would go out to the front again. Mother is at Hythe now with Gerald who is back for a period of instruction, but I did not quite gather if he had actually obtained a commission yet or not.

. . . The worst of the winter weather is over; very trying continually keeping the sea in these small craft. I cannot, in fact, remember having spent a more unpleasant winter.

Yours,
Fritz

CHAPTER FIVE

1916

TWO BROTHERS AND A CLOSE COUSIN IN FLANDERS FIELDS

He has died for the Empire and with his face to the enemy.
The Gods are not so kind to all men.

— Fritz Peters, on the death of his brother Gerald, 1916

The following letter reveals highlights of Fritz's life and career to date, his opinions on government and schooling, his intense dislike of traits of Americans and western Canadians, his love of Canada and his intention to enter politics in British Columbia after the war. His faith in the Empire was such that he believed mediocre politicians would somehow rise to greatness in an Empire-wide government.

FRITZ TO HIS FATHER FREDERICK   MARCH 16, 1916

Dear Father,

It is a long time since I have written to you. Letter writing is a pastime I do not much indulge in. You will doubtless ere this have heard from Mother concerning the probability of Jack being a prisoner in Belgium. Up to the time of writing there is no further news of him. I have recently paid a visit to the High Commissioner for Canada — Sir George Perley — whom you may know. To ask him to institute inquiries. He has approached the War Office on the matter and they are sending an inquiry to Germany, but I do not think much will come of it, nor for the matter of that did he. Belgium is, at present, closed and sealed to all outside enquiry and I think it unlikely that we will get news of Jack until peace is signed or unless he is sent to Germany. I think, though, that it is pretty well established that he is alive and a prisoner.

How is Prince Rupert these days? I take it money must be pretty hard to lay hands on. What do you think will be the state of things there, after the war, which I do not think will be prolonged much over the end of the year, if indeed this year does not see the conclusion of hostilities. That indeed it has lasted as long, we have to thank this precious government in England.

I wonder if the close of the war will see the beginning of an Imperial Government. What a wonderful thing that would be. Often have I pondered it. With it, organized in the proper manner, the empire would reach a power absolutely undreamt of, without it, and in the hands of these pettifogging politicians who at present govern England, in their spare moments giving a passing thought to the destinies of the Empire, there will inevitably be disintegration and Germany, as usual, will step in and take her Shylock's portion of the world's trade.

What, I think, is really wanted is the men in the colonies who are to step forward and make themselves heard on the matter, not only in their colony, but here strongly and forcibly at the root of this hopeless system of party government for our great Empire.

When this war is over, I am going in for politics in B.C. Rather an unpleasant life in many ways, but after all, whatever one may say, it is the end that matters and the road to it must be traversed as well as may be.

One thing this war has shown me, and that is how really intensely uninteresting naval warfare of today is. Personal enterprise becomes increasingly difficult, in fact one may say impossible. No one seems inclined to take risks — no doubt rightly, there may be little to justify them — but it does make life pretty dull, more or less.

Capacity to earn money? To a certain degree, no doubt.

But above all, a love of Empire, intense patriotism, a proper degree of respect for one's personal honour, a nice modesty, and, of course, religion.

What is your opinion of the growing Canadian (20-30 years) today? What is your candid and honest opinion?

I will give you mine, but before doing so I would have you consider of just what value can be attached to my opinion. I am now 27 and a half. First 11 years in Canada. A year at the Bedford Grammar School. Three years at Cordwalles — then one of the best preparatory schools in England.

I went to sea in the old Channel Fleet under Tug Wilson — one of England's greatest admirals — in 1906. Since then have been in Mediterranean and not unextensively in China under interesting conditions.

Then a year or more in Canada — the first few months nearly starving and glad to canvass a street, act as a beauty specialist or anything else that came my way. Then railway work in the interior.[i] Finally the war. Handicapped to a certain degree by absence from the Service, it would be stupid false modesty to say I have not done well. In my own line — destroyers — I have, perhaps through luck, done better than most and in it I know I am well considered by the powers that be.

All in all, I am not a fool. My experience has been more varied than most and my opinion in the councils of the wise man should at any rate have a hearing.

But above all I have a deep and I hope true love of Canada and perhaps some small idea of its future greatness and an undying firm belief in the absolute need of unity in the Empire. Do not, therefore, think that my remarks which follow are unduly "English" in their colouring or that I have joined what I would call the Anglicized Canadian type — a type for which I have little use.

The western Canadian, in my opinion, is a foolish braggart with small knowledge of the world and therefore lacking in all sense of proportion. Full of a ridiculous vanity, his conversation leaves one's mind as full of I-I-I's as does an hour in a railway train sweeping past a long line of telephone poles.

The so-called businessman, inflated beyond all belief in his own importance, the engineer, the woodsman, the street loafer, the tug master, type is not in Canada — and I don't think it is — How many decent Canadians go in for school mastering? Make it worthwhile for the English schoolmaster to come out.

There is no type of man for whom I have a greater respect than the English school master. He is underpaid; without capital he is unlikely ever to make much money; why does he do it? Many drift in and then stay because they like it. Because their life work is with boys of the right type. Can you imagine a team of boys from an English school throwing in their hand because they were being beaten — the idea is laughable. Each one would drop dead of exhaustion first. And why is this — answer: the teacher.

Early environment and later schooling count for more in my opinion than hereditary — which is merely an incentive — and aught else.

The Canadian soldier has pretty clearly shown that he has in the main the right qualities — the material is good, for the Lord's sake let the shaping of it in the future be better.

My eternal dread is that the remark of a traveled Englishman — and that remark referred to deeper things than mere superficial resemblance, which must always be similar — should one day be really true.

"I can see no difference", he said, "between the Canadian and a citizen of U.S.A."

Needless to say, I argued the point, but a man must be either ignorant or a fool if he cannot argue, and well too, on any point, for obviously there must be two sides to every question.

I am spending a few days leave with Helen Francklyn[ii] who sends her love. There is no news. This summer will be big with events. I think we have entered the last stretch; yes I think it is seconds out for the last round and like most last rounds it will be the fiercest. I think there will be another big sea fight before the business ends. I am afraid I shall not be in it. Still — ¿Quién sabe?[iii] Have not heard lately from New Denver (why in the name of the Lord was it called "New Denver" — is there such a poverty in the English language that we have to turn to the American?). No news else.

Yours,
Fritz

i.   By 'interior' he means the large part of British Columbia that is east and north of the Lower Mainland region that surrounds Vancouver.
ii. Helen Francklyn was one of Fred Peters' Cunard cousins.
iii. Meaning "who knows?"

Fritz's sister Helen and her family were living in the mining community of New Denver in the mountainous West Kootenay region of southeastern B.C., as her husband Ted Dewdney was transferred there as branch manager by the Bank of Montreal in early 1916. The community was originally settled by mostly Americans in the silver rush of the 1880s and early 1890s. The name 'New Denver' reflected the settlers' desire that it become as rich a mining centre as Denver in Colorado.

RESCUE OF SURVIVORS OF TORPEDOED FERRY

On March 24, 1916, the destroyer *Greyhound* under Fritz's command came to the rescue of survivors of the *SS Sussex* after the helpless ferry that carried passengers from England to Belgium was seriously damaged by a German torpedo, which killed at least 50 passengers. A subsequent torpedo aimed at *Greyhound* during the rescue narrowly missed its target. Although no Americans were among the dead, the incident enraged public opinion in the States and led to Germany's declaration of the Sussex Pledge, that limited the scope of its subsequent U-boat attacks.

Here, writing almost exactly a year after Jack disappeared in the Second Battle of Ypres, Fritz still believed Jack was alive and safe.

Dear Mother,

Many thanks for your letter the address of which I forgot to note and consequently am now without it. You did not say when you expected to leave Hythe to go to Folkestone. Am glad to hear that Gerald is getting along well.

All news of prisoners seems to point to little chance of getting news from any in Belgium. However I think it now quite certain that the end of the war will see Jack on his way home.

As for the war, it can end in one way only — unqualified victory for the Allies — if England so wills it. Sea power is playing in this war — as in bygone wars — the dominant role and Germany knows it. As Napoleon knew it. If Germany cannot bring England to her knees, she is lost — utterly and irretrievably lost — and none know it better than themselves. Are the lessons of history wasted? I think not. So long as England wills it, the end is certain and the end is victory. But the people are not yet awakened to the vastness of the effort required.

. . . I hate this letter-writing business.

No, you did not see me in London, where I have not been these past three months. As a matter of fact, on the day in question I was at sea.

Yours,
Fritz

After receiving so many assurances that Jack was alive, when Bertha was contacted by authorities at the end of May 1916 with news that Jack died at St. Julien a year earlier, she refused to believe it. Sadly, Pte. Jack Peters was still listed as missing in his father Fred Peters' obituary in newspapers in July 1919.

GERALD LEADS CHARGE IN MOUNT SORREL COUNTERATTACK

Gerald — who had told his sister Helen that he hated serving in the trenches of "Blasted Bloody Belgium" as a private with the Royal Victoria Rifles 24th Battalion through the winter of 1915–16 — got some good news in early 1916 when he was accepted into officer training. In April, he began as a lieutenant with the same 7th Battalion Jack served in, although few remembered Jack because of the almost complete turnover after the horrific casualties in the spring of 1915. Articles in the *Prince Rupert Daily News* reported that Lieut. Gerald Peters was training to expertly analyze captured German documents. The information was mailed by Bertha to her husband Fred. He took it to the newspaper editor, who was eager to run stories about a local boy fighting in the Great War.

Lt. Gerald Hamilton Peters, spring of 1916.

On June 2, 1916, Germans surprised the Allies with an attack that captured Mount Sorrel, which was east of Ypres, from Canadian forces. Success like this was unusual in the Great War because defenders usually had the advantage in any attack. The new commander of Canadian forces, Gen. Julian Byng — later to be a hero in the great Canadian victory at Vimy Ridge and serve as Governor General of Canada — felt Canadians must immediately launch a counterattack to get the high ground back from the Germans before they could establish strong defences.

According to the orders in place for British generals, Byng likely would have lost his command if he had not attacked. As a result, Gerald's unit was part of a hastily-planned advance on June 3rd, which never had any real chance of success. As happened so often in the war to troops on both sides, Gerald went over the top of his trench towards the enemy expecting to die, and he did. As Fritz noted later, without coordinated artillery support the offensive was doomed.

The following letter[1] from Bertha to a close older sister in Charlottetown shows her grief at the death of Gerald — which was obvious though not officially declared at the time — and her determination to get stories memorializing him in several newspapers.

BERTHA PETERS TO HER SISTER MARGARET LORD   JULY 6, 1916

Spreyton, Guildford

Darling Peg

So many thanks for several letters. I knew you would be sorry. It has been an overwhelming blow to me. It has crushed my very soul. I can't write about it. I have written a little account. I thought you might get it published in the Charlottetown paper.

. . . It's nearly killed me writing this out, but I did want to do it before he is forgotten. They are so quickly now. I had a great many letters and a lot of contradictory correspondence. From the front I have been careful only to put what has tallied and what I know to be fact. You will notice that I have not named any companies or battalions or officers' names. It's all so strictly forbidden now. If they do publish will you send Mary Abbott[i] a paper? You needn't tell people I wrote it. You could say it was sent you from England (except Maggie).[ii]

Please send me a paper if you do. Perhaps they won't think it worth printing. Florence[iii] and all of them have been so very kind. Nothing could be kinder. Goodbye dear. I am so glad Stewart is better.

Ever your loving
B.

i.   Mary Abbott was their sister in Montreal.
ii. She is referring to Fred Peters' unmarried sister Maggie in Charlottetown, with whom she and her family were very close.
iii. Her sister Florence Poole, at whose home in Guildford she was staying at the time.

Despite what appears to be positive news in the letter about the health of Margaret's six-year-old grandson Stewart MacDonald, the boy died later in July 1916 from a botched appendix operation. Health care on the home front suffered because of war demands.

Fritz wrote to his mother on the same day she wrote to her sister Margaret. He was still holding out hope that Gerald was alive.

FRITZ TO HIS MOTHER BERTHA   JULY 5, 1916

My Dear Mother

I have just received your letter. I wish I could meet Captain Ford. Do you know where he could be found? He does not give much hope for Gerald, but I cannot think that there is no hope.

If Gerald was in a ditch presumably he managed to crawl there. This would afford protection from shell fire — except a direct hit. Nor am I very clear as to whether his company held the ground beyond where G. fell. If they went on and dug themselves in beyond where G. fell — Gerald thus being in our lines — then it does not look hopeful, but on this point Capt. Ford does not seem very clear.

I think this makes all the difference. If Gerald fell and we finally left this ground so that Gerald was left — as I think he probably was — in no man's land, then I think it is quite possible that he might be taken by a German stretcher party. The Huns send out their stretcher parties in the same way we do and it is quite conceivable that seeing an officer there they would take him prisoner. If our stretcher party could find no signs of Gerald, it is very unlikely that he is killed and nothing that anyone can tell me will convince me otherwise. His position where he fell would surely be known almost exactly and only a direct hit right in the ditch itself would entirely wipe him out and this is unlikely.

I am glad Gerald was first over the parapet. I am glad it was a counterattack and not merely another trench casualty. Poor old Jelly. I wonder if he did think of me, as he got over the parapet. I should be proud if he did.

Poor Mother, this is very hard for you, but — through it all — I do not give up hope. I am writing to a Canadian surgeon — a Vancouver man whom I know very well and who will I am certain make the fullest possible enquiries as to Gerald being in one of our hospitals.

Ever yours,
Fritz

A few weeks after Gerald was reported missing and almost certainly killed, Fritz travelled to the Ypres Salient to investigate what happened to Gerald, responding to desperate demands for information from his mother.

FRITZ TO HIS MOTHER BERTHA   JULY 23, 1916

H.M.S. Greyhound

My Dear Mother,

I have just returned from 7th Battalion and it is bad news that I bring with me. Poor old Jelly[i] was killed on June 3rd and his body has been recovered. Everything possible was done to get him in, but he must have attempted to crash in himself and been killed in the attempt.

At present the exact location of his grave is unknown as he was found and buried by PPLI.[ii]

Shortly the 7th will be close to them and the Major now commanding has promised to write me at once exactly where he has been buried and to see cross put up.

It is very hard for you. His personal effects found on him will be sent to you shortly. I could not get them. His company commander (not then commanding) searched from 9 p.m. until daylight that night. Gerald must probably have been struck and instantly killed by a shell.

Well, Mother, what words of comfort can I offer? For you it is the hardest part. It is the price of Empire. I pray God I fall in the same manner with my face to the enemy. I will write you tomorrow the fullest details, though there is little to add, but must mail this now. This will probably be your first word.

Yours ever,
Fritz

i.   Family nickname for Gerald.
ii. Princess Patricia's Canadian Light Infantry, also abbreviated PPCLI.

At about the same time, Fritz wrote to his sister Helen in Canada filling her in on what happened to Gerald. He reminded her that nothing was more important than "King and Empire".

My Diegle Hagen,[i]

This is sad news about poor old Jelly. I suppose you will have heard by now that he has been killed. I am but shortly returned from a visit to the 7th Battalion. I found them in their rest camp not far from Ypres. They were to return to reserve trenches the next night. Word had then just come through from the regiment who relieved them (the PPCLI) that Gerald's body had been discovered.

It is a sickening business — the more so for poor Mother. She had been nearly distracted by different letters she had received, all more or less contradictory, and had made up her mind that Gerald could have been saved if only someone had taken the trouble to try and get him.

Well, I saw them all — all that were left and in justice to them, I don't think it their fault that G. wasn't got in. I will give you the story as I know it:

The 7th Battalion were ordered to make a counterattack on the morning of 3 June. It was doomed to failure before they started, with no artillery preparation, but was apparently necessary to show the Huns that they could not come on.

At 7:30 a.m. they commenced the attack — Gerald's company supporting 2 or 4, I forget which. Enfiladed by machine guns it was repulsed. Gerald got about 80 yards when he was hit and rolled over into a trench or rather a sap. By this time the attack had failed and everyone had taken cover and was retreating to our trench.

Gerald was wounded through the wrist, leg and shoulder — all slight flesh wounds but apparently sufficiently bad to keep him from crawling in at once. His wounds were dressed and he was put in a good position in the sap — being about 3 inches below surface.

To carry him in was impossible as he would have been exposed and at once killed. Where he was, he was entirely safe from rifle fire and not many shells were falling in the middle of No Man's Land, nearly all were falling on our trench.

Meanwhile what was left of the battalion was slowly creeping back. Barton saw Gerald about 9 a.m. and gave him a flask of rum. Captain Saunders — who told me most and who had written me before — left Gerald at 10 a.m. giving him a bottle of water and biscuits and promising to get him in that night. Gerald was quite all right then. Carstairs was the last to see him I suppose about noon (I have not seen Carstairs) and after that the rest must be surmise.

At 9 p.m. Saunders went out and straight to the spot — the spot itself was undamaged by shell, but no signs of Gerald. Saunders was out until

1:30 a.m. and got in 25 wounded. I don't think he could have done more. He saw no signs of Gerald.

If only Gerald had waited he would undoubtedly have been saved. Probably he rallied and thought he would crawl in as many of the wounded did during the day.

Perhaps he exposed himself, or went the wrong way or a stray shell. Suffice it, that he never got in. The Major, now commanding 7th Battalion, has promised me the exact location of his grave and a cross to be put up. Also to see how far he did get.

It is very heartbreaking. He was so keen to do great things. He has died for the Empire and with his face to the enemy and the Gods are not so kind to all men. I shall visit his grave as soon as the war is over or perhaps earlier. Standing there that afternoon in the rest camp with a blazing sun overhead and the green fields around, there was little of war save the sound of a bombing party practicing and the occasional drone of some passing aeroplane.

The regiment was passing the afternoon with a boxing competition — the regulation ring and the men four deep around it, I sharing an old box with the Major (Gardiner by name) and I couldn't help thinking how often old Jack must have been doing just the same and then Jelly. It made me very sad. Poor old Jack — I don't see how one can keep up the farce of hoping. No, for them both the soldier's grave in the firing line and for us the stiff upper lip and the thought that it is for the Empire.

Poor Mother — I don't know what she will do. She was so bound up in Gerald. I want her now to go out to you for a few months and then to come back to England until the war is over. She can never go back to Prince Rupert. She would lose her reason if she did. Of that I am sure.

The casualties are very heavy these days. Few people are unaffected. I was very sorry Hubert Leatham[ii] *was killed and also both the Laurences.*

Give my chin chin to Ted. I hope my niece is well. I was very sorry to hear you had been laid up during the winter with throat trouble.

Heavens what a transitory business life is! Consider it, one day after another, a month, a year — slide by. Here, Helen, you are twenty-nine and I twenty-seven. A brief space — old age — death.

A death in action — surely if we are judged for the vast eternity by this brief mortal span — must be something.

Poor old Father — alone in Prince Rupert. Yes, the war has hit us pretty hard.

But what is it, Hagen, in the balance? There is only one thing — the King and Empire.

Yours,
Fritz

i. Family nickname for sister Helen.
ii. John Sandford Leatham of the Canadian 13th Battalion died June 12, 1916, at Ypres.

Gerald's grave turned out to be short-term, as the cemetery was destroyed by subsequent shelling and changes in control of territory. Gerald joined brother Jack among the thousands of soldiers who died in Flanders with unidentified remains. About four months after Gerald's death, Fred Peters received a letter from Sergeant-Major Dawson who was recovering in hospital from wounds suffered in the Mount Sorrel action. Dawson said he saw Gerald drop about 60 yards towards the objective 700 yards away. "He was the coolest boy I think I have ever seen," Dawson wrote. Gerald was "as game as a lion and as gentle as a lamb. His life was short, but, by God, he was a man."[2]

After moving to London and writing a barrage of letters from the Windsor Hotel to everyone she could think of about Gerald's status, Bertha went to Guildford again to stay at her sister Florence Poole's house before returning to Canada in November 1916.

In the following letter, Fritz mentions a Victoria Cross awarded to a British pilot, Lt. William Leefe Robinson, for shooting down a German Zeppelin airship. Zeppelins were dropping bombs on targets in England. On Sept. 3, 1916, Robinson became the first British flyer to shoot down a zeppelin, and the first to earn a VC for action over Britain.

FRITZ TO HIS MOTHER BERTHA   SEPTEMBER 7, 1916

Dear Mother,

Of course I don't mind you leaving the Windsor. I quite agree it is the closest approach to a tomb that I know. I like the smoking room and as a matter of fact I enjoy the walk across the park in the morning to the haunts of leisure in Picadilly.

Don't get a doll for Helen's baby. I am getting something which I will get you to take out. I don't see why you shouldn't change your mind about going out. Even I — paragon of all virtues — change my mind occasionally.

On the other hand, I expect I could send you £50 early next year if you want to come back. Really I think it is a matter of your inclination. I should think the change for a few months would do you good.

I, too, am hopeful about Jack.

Hear there is little news. I have written about Gerald, but I don't hold out much hope of further information. Amongst the thousand other queries, time quickly put aside details, nor is it to be wondered at.

I read Father's speech with much interest. Poor old Father — he must feel pretty sad at times. I thought the speech good — of course the usual thundering type — Father never went in for half measures — the more power to his elbow. Truly "a might have been" but if it comes to that there are thousands more in this wicked world.

The war goes on. I am hopeful of an earlier finish than most people anticipate, but really I have nothing to go on.

I must get you to take some books out to Helen. One can get nearly anything worth reading these days on at the most a shilling.

I wish I could come up for a night and take you to something just to cheer you up, but I fear at the moment it is impossible.

It is good work this Zeppelin being brought down. The pilot comes out of it pretty well. V.C. and the best part of four thousand jimmies.

My old friend Powell has just returned to the front — this time commanding a battery. He was before in the Seaforths and came back with nothing worse than a slight flesh wound.

> *Your son,*
> *Fritz*

Below Fritz responds to Bertha's plan to visit her daughter Helen in B.C., where he has fond memories of the mountains.

FRITZ TO HIS MOTHER BERTHA   SEPTEMBER 26, 1916

My Dear Mother,

Your time grows short now. I wonder if you have had your night's sleep disturbed lately by these Zepps. Life here has been pretty busy. In fact I have — save for 24 hours off — had my hands full since I left you. Well I wish I were bound once more for the far West — for the deep stillness of the mountains — alone a million miles from the rush and hubbub of the world — and just the vast eternity of space above you and the incredible solitude of the mountains around you.

I wonder if I shall see those slopes again in this brief mortal span.

I do hope Butler has turned up to see you off. I wish it were possible that I could. Probably when you shove off from the famous Prince's Landing Slope I shall also be on the deep.

There is little to say. My love to Helen and Ted and to the young chee-ild a kiss and then a sound spanking — just to keep her in order.

I give the war twelve months more to run, but I think before then I shall see you in England again with Helen.

Yours ever,
Fritz

A COUSIN'S COURT MARTIAL

In Bertha's mind, there was only one thing worse than losing a son in battle — and it was about to happen to her sister Florence's son. Born in Nova Scotia in 1885, Eric Skeffington Poole served in the Halifax Rifles militia in the early 1900s before moving with his parents to England in about 1905. Fritz Peters knew Eric well from regular visits between the Peters and Poole families before Fritz's family moved west. He joined the British Army as a driver in October 1914 and by 1916 was a 2nd Lieutenant with the 11th Battalion of the West Yorkshire Regiment. Eric came out of the Battle of the Somme in July 1916 with pronounced symptoms of what was then called 'shell shock'. He had recurring periods of confusion after returning from medical treatment, and then on October 5, 1916, wandered away from his platoon at the front. Jack Peters had mentioned his concern for cousin Eric's health in his letters home in December 1914 when Eric was in hospital "as a result of trench digging on a wet night" and again in April 1915, which would indicate he had longstanding health issues. A day after being found away from his unit in a confused state, Eric was arrested by military police and faced a court martial for desertion. Despite evidence that he was still suffering from shell shock — or what might today be termed Post-Traumatic Stress Disorder — which made him anxious and confused, he was found guilty and sentenced to death.

NO MERCY FROM HAIG

British Field Marshal Douglas Haig could have commuted his sentence but chose to make an example of him to demonstrate throughout the ranks that officers were subject to the same rules for desertion as enlisted men.[3]

On December 16, 1916, Eric was shot at dawn by a firing squad at Poperinghe, Belgium, about 10 miles from where his cousins Jack and Gerald Peters recently died in battle. His gravestone in Poperinghe Cemetery does not mention that he died by execution. He was the first of three British officers in the war to be executed for desertion. While the court martial was under way, Bertha was staying at the Poole residence and preparing for her return to Canada.

With Eric's father Henry Poole seriously ill in hospital, his wife Florence worried that hearing of Eric's troubles would kill his father. The War Office agreed not to put out any information on the circumstances of his death. It appears Florence had an arrangement with authorities that the family would not contest the verdict if they did not publicize Eric's conviction and execution. The Poole family apparently also kept Eric's execution secret from most of their extended family. Helen Dewdney never mentioned it to her children or even in her private family history notes describing her Poole cousins, so it is possible she never knew of it. Florence's sister Margaret Lord in Charlottetown made no mention of it in her personal diaries, so she may have been kept in the dark about it too. She and others in the family may have thought that Eric died in war action like so many others. Bertha likely knew because she was staying at the Poole house when the ordeal began. She may have told Fritz, or he may have heard about it as a naval officer familiar with military reports. None of the Peters family records say anything about Eric's execution.

In the following letters written by Fritz to his mother in late 1916, he does not mention his cousin Eric's court martial, probably because he spent this period mostly at sea and was therefore unaware of what was happening.

He writes here shortly after taking command of the destroyer HMS *Christopher* in Chatham.

FRITZ TO HIS MOTHER BERTHA   OCTOBER 6, 1916

My Dear Mother,

Have been really too busy to write before or now at any length. What is the name of the ship that you will be crossing in on November 2nd? Where have you decided to stay in London? There will be no chance at all for me to see you before you leave.

One is reminded that the winter is approaching again. It is a blessing to find one's self once again in a seaworthy craft. At present as is usual in recommissioning everything is upside down. Time is the only cure. Another month or so will effect much.

I thought of you on the 29th as plunging your way westward into the Atlantic[i] — westward, into the far, far West with the setting sun and the great mountains sweeping down into the lakes.

I had a letter from Father a few days ago but it did not contain any news of interest.

I spent a day last month at Windermere. The first time that I had been in the Lake district in England — very quiet and very much at peace. A beautiful day and the lake like a mill pond. Miles away from war, or rumour of war.

Nothing much of interest to tell you. Have hardly seen a paper these past five days.

Yes, London is a great place to wander aimlessly about. Think of the countless thousands, nay millions, who have hurried to and fro like a hive of busy bees. Each with their own small constellations, their hopes and fears, their joys and sorrows, today they're here and tomorrow they're gone.

Truly life is a strange proposition.

Yours,
Fritz

i.   Bertha was originally scheduled to leave for Canada in late September, but her voyage home was postponed by about six weeks.

In the following letter, Fritz expresses relief at taking command of a newer and faster ship. Launched in 1912, the destroyer HMS *Christopher* had maximum speed of 32 knots.[4]

FRITZ TO HIS MOTHER BERTHA   OCTOBER 15, 1916

My Dear Mother,

It is some time since I have heard from you. I hope you're alright. Are you in London now or still with Aunt Florence?

I have been very busy these past three weeks. It is an irksome business settling down in a new ship though interesting, really, when it is one's own. There is always the fear that one may be given one's opportunity too soon — before you are so organized as to make the very best of it. Still, it is a great thing to have a decent craft again after a perishing thirty knotter. Another winter in the Greyhound would have driven me to drink or suicide or both.

I had a letter from Father the other day, but it did not contain anything worth recording. The main drawback to this place is that one gets no leave to speak of. I look forward really to a pretty quiet winter.

You have not chosen a very good month to cross the Atlantic. I hope you will find Helen well. I should think that in one of the Bank's houses[i] you should not suffer from cold. I must send something out to the young brat, but my brain — undoubtedly great though it is — always refuses to work when faced with a problem of this nature. My thoughts revolve around the tiger, but really it is a waste of money to spend it on a toy that will probably be out of action within a week.

I wonder what Helen will find to do during the winter months — now if she were a huntress she might out into the mountains with the infant strapped on her back, to hunt the lone grey wolf — but perhaps that would not appeal to her.

Have you heard lately from the Mellishes? It is really a long time since I have seen them. Nearly two years — at Hodsock at any rate.

This cursed train service is so damnably bad that I might as well be in Timbuktoo — as hope to get anywhere in reasonable time even if one would get away. What boat are you now going to cross by and when does she sail and when is she due in Montreal?

Write me your movements.

Yours truly,
Fritz

i. The Bank of Montreal provided houses for its branch managers in each community. While this arrangement enabled the manager to save on housing costs, it also gave senior management the ability to move managers around as they saw fit at short notice.

BERTHA COULD NOT BEAR TO RETURN TO PRINCE RUPERT HOME

Returning by steamship from England in November 1916, a grieving mother was still distraught over Gerald's death and the continuing uncertainty, at least in her mind, about Jack's fate. She appears to have never returned to the family home in Prince Rupert, as she — as well as Fritz and Helen — feared she would be overwhelmed with grief from encountering memories in the house of her beloved son Gerald. Instead, she stayed with daughter Helen's family, an arrangement that continued for the next three decades. Her husband Fred was left to manage on his own in the isolated coastal port.

Below, Fritz writes approvingly of a change two days earlier in the British government. On December 7, 1916, Herbert Asquith was replaced as Britain's prime minister by David Lloyd George, reflecting the change in the political environment from "business as usual" and protection of the status quo to "total war", phrases that were in common usage in Britain at the time.[5]

My Dear Mother,

I trust long ere this reaches you that you will have arrived at New Denver. It sounds as though one ought to put Kansas or Washington or something equally ill-sounding after it. I wonder who was the genius responsible for such an ill-chosen name. Long since this I meant to have written you, but of a truth I have little time for writing and what small time I have is entirely engrossed in the filling of voluminous registers — an appalling pile of documents requiring my illustrious signature stands on my left, and what I should be doing is to stretch my truly weary limbs on an inviting brink or lose myself in the wonders, the mysteries of a sweet dreamland.

I hope you wrote me from Montreal. Did my namesake[i] worry you at all on the old Atlantic? They cause me many sleepless hours. God help the one I meet — he will receive scant mercy from yours truly.

How did you find Helen and Ted and the small child? I forget if you got her a doll from me. I grieve I omitted in the maze of a vast series of financial operations to get her the tiger. She has my love and best wishes.

I got your two telegrams about five days after you had sailed. During the intervening period I was thrashing this perishing ocean.

I return you Swann's letter. I have written him and can hardly express an opinion of much value until I hear from him. I attach small hope to his letter. If Jack was in Germany, then he would be able to communicate.

Lieut. Robinson of the 49th Battalion found Gerald's body. Gerald was buried by Captain Clark of P.P.C.L.I.

The war must now be nearing its final stage. I should think another two years should bring it to a termination. One gets out of touch going for so long without a paper. Certainly some days ago it looked as though Asquith, that hat peg for so much abuse, must really go.

This is a wonderful period. A hundred years hence, it will be the cause of much study, many laboured essays and otherwise wasting of that valuable commodity — ink — and no one can say that the end is in sight and that the scales have gone down to the winner. Already I can hear the rush of feet along the upper deck. What will it be? A man with a large fat cheque for me? I think not. I am no prophet, but it will be something in this wise — "Raise steam with utmost dispatch and report when ready!" I wish I too could step further and view the great mountains and the great lakes.

Just to watch the sun sink, and the moon flood all the still world with her splendour. If, indeed, there is a heaven above, it must be fashioned in this manner.

By the way, have you received a volume of letters from the CPR addressed Mrs. F. Peters. Letters from one, two — five different ships, was it not. I flatter myself they were rather well done and like the great artist I am, I never once repeated myself. I am thinking of starting a school — hints on how to write letters to the departing guest — somewhat in that line.

Yours,
Fritz

i. He means Germans, who were often called 'Fritz' like
    his nickname.

Writing in late 1916, Fritz reflects on Admiral Nelson's navy of the previous century and wonders how the Great War will be remembered a century in the future.

FRITZ TO HIS MOTHER BERTHA   DECEMBER 16, 1916

My Dear Mother,

I was awfully glad to get your letter to say that you were arrived in the St. Lawrence. I hope you had a good trip across Canada and found Helen and her family in good form. I shall be interested to hear what you think of New Denver. I suppose too much of real nature about it for your likings. I suppose you will have seen Aunt Mim in Montreal. By the way, what has happened to Maggie Peters?[i] One never hears of her these days — the Auntie Na that in P.E.I. we were so fond of.

Here life goes on as usual. These sweeping changes in the Government seem all for the good. For pure vigour, we have today a very healthy collection of leaders. I think now, in truth, it will be death or glory, and war was never yet successfully waged without risks and probably never will be.

There is extraordinarily little to tell you. I hope we shall spend Christmas at sea. It is a wretched day in harbour especially in war time.

This sea business is terribly dull, a great deal of sea time with perishing little to show for it. Twas ever thus. A hundred odd years ago the frigates of old were scouring the channel. Nelson's Mediterranean fleet were keeping their ceaseless vigil off Toulon in the Gulf of Lyons where rules the worst weather in the world — scarce three fine days in as many months. Imagine it in the old three-decker — the continual strain of shops short of all supplies. The terrible weather, the ceaseless, utter monotony beside which today one's own boredom fades into insignificance.

Wonderful to think of it all — England facing the world — France usurping Germany's position of today. Think of the countless ships that have ploughed their way through the Channel — think of the galleons laden with gold — of the great convoys of merchantmen and then of the fleet of the ships of the line — that barrier which today as then stands solid as a rock between England and her enemies.

Truly it is a great tradition that lies behind the Navy of England.

And I wonder where we were then and where we will be in 2016.

Some passable weather considering the time of the year. I must now settle down to a few diplomatic letters to my various tradesmen, a letter of Christmas greeting to my banker . . . and a host of letters to various others, not to speak of some 12 different reports as to why I have done this and why I have not done that, and in the end I shall pick up a book and enter a world far from these maudlin things and so do none of them.

Good night. I think of you in the shadow of the mountains.

Yours,
Fritz

i. Fred's sister Margaret Laura Peters (1855 – 1935) never married and still lived in Charlottetown.

Chapter Six

1917 – 1918
Hunting U-boats and Rescuing Stricken Sailors

If I had been censured every time I have run my ship, or fleets under my command, into great danger, I should have long ago been out of the service and never in the House of Peers.

— Lord Admiral Horatio Nelson, 1805

At the start of 1917, Fritz was in command of HMS *Christopher* and regularly writing to his mother, who continued living with the Dewdney family in New Denver, B.C., unable to bear to return to the family home in Prince Rupert filled with memories of her dead sons.

FRITZ TO HIS MOTHER BERTHA   JANUARY 16, 1917

My Dear Mother,

Hope you're all well. Life going on here much as usual, which means highly monotonous. The war is entering an interesting phase. This I hope will be the year of victory and 1918 rout to the Huns. I don't see how we can predict anything until we have seen what happens on the Western Front this summer. Beat them then and they are at our mercy.

Am looking forward to a few days leave in February. I suppose now I will see the war to an end in this craft, much as I would like a new one. My seniority is wrong — too junior for anything good.

How is Helen and whatever the brat is called? How long does Ted expect to remain at New Denver before getting a shift somewhere else? It must be a trial being unable to get any servants. Nuisance moving from one house to another. Will Ted go to Victoria or anywhere like that soon, think you?

I have not heard from Father for many moons. Winter is with us. Pretty cold and not very pleasant at sea. I dislike cold weather at sea most intensely. The water has that chill which, pleasant enough in the cold bath of the morning, gets monotonous through excess. I think I am going to write a play this year just to collect a few of those so necessary shekels. Well, there will be "some" slaughter this spring. I take it my share in this perishing war is over . . . . Who can tell? Love to all.

Yours,
F.T.P.

P.S. By the way, when is my young niece's birthday?
P.P.S. You have not answered my query as to the ice boat, which it is my intention to bring with me.

Lt. Frederic Thornton Peters wearing the Messina Earthquake Medal.

In the following letter to his mother, Fritz mentions in a terse sentence that he was sorry that Eric had died. The sentence was immediately after a comment that censors were reading all of her letters, which may have been a hint to Bertha to be very careful with anything she says about Eric in such a sensitive environment. The war had been going badly for the Allies and political and military leaders were terrified of mutinies, as happened in the French army later in 1917. This is the only mention of the death of cousin Eric Poole in any of the Peters Family Letters. Eric was among 345 British soldiers shot by firing squads, compared to only 48 German soldiers tried and executed in the same war. Field Marshal Haig believed executions were essential for maintaining discipline. British soldiers had no right to appeal a death sentence, and information about military execution proceedings was kept secret, even from next-of-kin and the House of Commons.[1]

FRITZ TO HIS MOTHER BERTHA   FEBRUARY 10, 1917

I am owing you a letter for some time, but have little leisure either in or out of harbour. You ask me concerning bridge. I should think Bascule was as good as any. As far as I remember, I once sent you a book on bridge, which if my memory serves me right, I carefully selected from a bookstall at Paddington Station. You said, too, it was no good — base ingratitude. Never mind, undaunted, I will send you another one.

Bridge, in any case, depends a good deal on luck — given players of equal skill, there is 80% luck in the business.

I was reading an article in the Strand magazine for February on pirate bridge — an idea apparently originating — not with the Hun — but with the author. Glancing casually over it, it seemed as though it might prove amusing.

By the way, a question I have asked several times remains still unanswered — what is the birthday of the small girl Evelyn?

I notice nowadays all your letters are opened by the Censor.

I was sorry to hear Eric Poole has been killed.

Little of interest. Do you ever hear from Father these days? He seldom writes to me, but on the other hand I cannot pretend to carrying on any vast correspondence with him.

I wish I could get some booty out of this cursed war. I see one of our submarine people has in a claim for £31,000 for sinking a Turkish troopship. I hope he gets it, but expect that the noble Lord of the Treasury will put a healthy spoke in his calculations. A cheque for a small sum of that nature would be highly diverting.

Love to all.

Yours,
Fritz

In the following letter, Fritz expresses interest in becoming a schoolmaster after the war and mentions discussing the profession with a fellow named Harvey. Fritz does not appear to be aware that his brother Jack Peters served under Capt. R.V. Harvey in the 7th B.C. Battalion. Injured and taken prisoner in the Second Battle of Ypres, Harvey died later in a German P.O.W. camp.

Fritz blames poor schooling for an incident before the war in Vancouver where members of a rugby team contemplated quitting a game when they were far behind in points. He expresses interest in researching Canadian history in England, likely encouraged by his grandfather John Hamilton Gray's status as a Father of Confederation.

FRITZ TO HIS FATHER FREDERICK   MARCH 3, 1917

The Cottage, Hambrook, Bristol
My Dear Father,

Very many thanks for your letter which I received some time ago. I shall be enormously obliged if you will send me the names of the books that I shall require to study Canadian politics. If circumstances permit I shall most certainly make a close study of the documents in the British Museum relating to the Confederation, before returning to Canada. Your views on history are my own. The hackneyed saying "there is nothing new under the sun" is certainly largely borne out by a study of history and truly what can be more interesting than the lives of the great men of the past. Yet history to the majority of men is a closed book — closed when the school days are over and gone.

Myself, I have but lately given any thought or study to the matter.

As you say, there must be many questions in Canada, as well as else-where in Empire, that will require immediate settlement, but I suppose I could hardly hope to take an active part in politics before the seven years after the war, during which period I would hope to make sufficient to be able to be free to devote myself entirely to politics.

To my way of thinking, the most pressing question in Canada today is the question of teaching in the schools.

I have lately made friends with a very worthy fellow who is a partner in a firm in London whose business it is to supply school masters etc to schools principally in England but also to the colonies. He has supplied some six schools in Canada with masters — perhaps not absolutely first class, but at any rate very good — good enough for the "Clifton" type say of English public school. These schools — staffed principally by English school masters — are run on English public school lines and have been very successful from a moneymaking point of view. What type of person they turn out I don't know, but should immensely like to know. In particular, there was one at Vancouver (I think) called University College run by an Englishman by name of Harvey — a most excellent fellow I believe. Aged perhaps 43, he volunteered and was killed early in the war and I do not know what has happened to the school. Now these as I say are some half dozen schools of I should think an excellent type, but what of the remainder? What of the state schools — they are run by government are they not?

After all, what do you want to gain most by education? Knowledge — well, any type of school master can impart that the hotel employee, the journalist, one and all are tarred with a hideous coat of vanity, and what is the reason of it? What can it be but the early schooling.

I remember an incident — I shall not easily forget it — a game of rugger in Vancouver. One side a team of very decent fellows for whom I occasionally turned out when circumstances permitted and the other a team of boys from a Canadian school. This team of boys were outplayed and being badly beaten. Half way through the second half they got fed up and decided to give up the game. There was much talk and finally they did play it out, but imagine the idea even being considered by a team of decent boys!

Bah — the thought of it makes me vomit.

That is, I presume (from the present result) the type of school that is turning out the Western citizen of today.

No doubt the war will do much, but future education will do a deal more and it must — unless you would have Canada a second United States — devoid of anything, honour or aught else, save an overwhelming self-conceit. God forbid it.

And after all his talk, the Western Canadian is not a very first-class specimen of humanity — give him many points — self-reliance, a certain ability to do things, but lacking largely in truth or personal honour and without these two, the rest are just sawdust in the mouth.

This enormous self-conceit will be a stumbling block in the way of any just system of Imperial representation, which must come, and I would be well pleased to see it uprooted and the seeds of a more becoming modesty sown in its place.

Heavens, it's a wonderful country. B.C. will one day take its place in the councils of Empire, but from its present population that place would be as well-filled by one of those damned money grubbers below the border, whose end and aim in life is the dollar — a goal shared far too largely by the Western Canadians.

Such are my views — I would admit them to few, but such they are and I pray that one day I may be able to alter them.

I should be more than interested to hear yours, not your newspaper views but what you really think on the matter.

The remedy just lie in the staffs of the schools. Make your teachers good — instilled with the right principles — and the rest will follow...

[rest of letter missing]

Here, Fritz seems to be bored and frustrated with life at sea between conflicts. The letter shows that, unlike his brothers Gerald and Jack who were abstainers, Fritz enjoyed a good drink or two in the navy tradition. Once again, he asks for the birthday of his three-year-old niece Eve, a detail that was either missed in previous letters by his correspondents or forgotten by Fritz after being told.

FRITZ TO HIS MOTHER BERTHA   MARCH 6, 1917

Dear Mother,

I am afraid it is a long time since I last wrote. How is Helen? Life here continues much the same as ever. A good deal of sea time and not much tangible result. I am rather tired of being a miserable pawn in the game and would like to find myself suddenly shot up into one of the positions of power — just to feel the levers of mighty happenings in one's grasp — well who knows one day — if I am not dead of drink or some other pleasant complaint — probably a swollen liver. I don't think I am a very pleasant person to serve under.

There is deuced little to say. I have chewed off half my pen and come to the undoubted conclusion that there is nothing to say. What I would like is a gramophone which you just talk into — it records the talking — and then these priceless words of wisdom are thrust into the post and hence you from your gramophone can hear my sweet voice calling as Harry Tate[i] — the immortal — would have it.

Just think of the trouble you'd save — think of the economy in ink.

I am quite disgusted to hear this wretched lake never freezes. What is the good of a lake that does not freeze? I take it is very deep. The Okanagan Lake used to freeze, did it not?

Yes, money or the lack of it, is rather a curse at times. I wonder if yours truly will die with many millions. I don't think so.

I'm glad the young chee-ild shows character. I think she will turn out a real flier. I hope so.

Love to all. When is the child's birthday? This, my dear Mother, is the fifteenth time of asking.

Yours,
Fritz

i.   Harry Tate (1872 – 1940) was a Scottish comedian who performed in music halls and films.

The U-boat war in the Atlantic was getting increasingly desperate in early 1917, to the point that passenger liners were included as targets for German subs. Here, Fritz advises his mother of the danger of travel across the Atlantic because of U-boats.

FRITZ TO HIS MOTHER BERTHA   MARCH 25, 1917

Hodsock Priory, Worksop

My Dear Mother,

I am enjoying a few days leave and am at present at Hodsock where everyone is well and much the same as ever. Few changes here save in the farm labourer — largely replaced by women. Blustery weather for March — snow and northerly winds, which feel their way to the backbone.
Shall later this week pay the Francklyns a visit.
I hope Helen and her family are all right.
Little news from these parts that will interest you. I hope you receive the "Weekly Times" fairly regularly. Posts abroad now are not highly reliable and letters from Canada are a long time in the coming. The Christopher goes strong. I suppose that unless the unexpected happens, I shall see the business through in her. One is badly placed for seniority which puts one out of the running for a more amusing flotilla.
You certainly will not be able to return to England before the war is over. To cross the Atlantic during the present time is a thing I should not care to see you attempt.
However, I think the end of this summer will give one some more definite idea as to how the war is going to terminate. Certainly the social problems that will as a matter of course follow any peace proceedings will take a good deal of settling — but first and foremost — to finish the war . . .
This recent German retreat must give one a clearer idea as to the fate of the invaded territory. How can we in England realize the true meaning of the frightfulness of war until the country has been invaded — which pray God it never will be.
Love to all.

Yours,
Fritz

BROTHER NOEL ENTERS FORESTRY CORPS

In May 1917, with authorities desperate for new recruits, Noel Peters was accepted in the Canadian Forestry Corps which conducted logging in Britain and France to meet the need for wood in the war. The idea was to bring Canadian loggers to Britain and France to harvest local wood for the war effort, rather than logging in Canada and sending the loads across the Atlantic on ships vulnerable to U-boat attacks.

The other positive news for the family on the home front was the birth in May 1917 in New Denver of Helen's son Frederic Hamilton Bruce Dewdney, who throughout his life would be known as 'Peter'. One of the quirks of the family was to call children by names different from their registered name. As an adult, he had his second middle name legally changed from Bruce to Peter. No one ever knew him as Frederic.

The baby boy was named Frederic after his uncle Fritz, and Fritz agreed to be his godfather. One of Peter Dewdney's great regrets was never meeting his heroic uncle, godfather and namesake. Following Fritz's example, Peter served in the Royal Canadian Navy in the Second World War on anti-U-boat patrols off the east coast of Canada and towards the Caribbean.

Here, Fritz expresses regrets at the death of his uncle Henry Skeffington Poole, who died on March 31, 1917 at 73. He was well-known as a mining engineer and administrator in England and Canada's Maritimes.

FRITZ TO HIS MOTHER BERTHA   JUNE 2, 1917

Dear Mother,

Many thanks for your letter of May 4th which I have just received. I am delighted to hear this news of Helen and of course I should be equally delighted to be his Godfather. Be careful to spell his name without the "k" — Frederic — saves ink — war economy. Anyhow it's how I spell mine. How old is Evelyn? What do you call her? I suppose the boy will be called Fred. It really is splendid and the family right too, to be fine healthy specimens of humanity . . .

Life here much as usual. We do a great deal of sea time in fact we live there entirely and at times I get very bored. Wish I had joined the New Army or the flying corps and see something of war.

Yes it was sad to hear of Uncle Henry's death — a most honourable man. Kindness itself — but he was full of years and after all what is this life of one's but a transitory flight across a brief space of time and then into the vast eternity of life beyond. Who but a fool can believe in nothing and if one does believe in Christianity surely the sorrows of this life are but short lived in the certainty of reunion in the next.

If one doesn't believe in Christianity, well the devil help us because no one else will . . .

Yours,
Fritz

Hearing from his mother about the wonderful scenery and peacefulness of New Denver and the Slocan Valley got Fritz thinking about living near water after the war.

FRITZ TO HIS MOTHER BERTHA   JULY 12, 1917

Dear Mother,

I am certainly a poor correspondent, but can the leopard change his spots? I am sorry to hear Helen is still poorly.

I am distressed to hear that the lake does not freeze. This is certainly a great drawback. The Okanagan lakes used to freeze.

I suppose this is deeper. To my mind nothing is so refreshing as living beside water.

The sea I think for preference if the coast line is an attractive one such as Cornwall or Italy or indeed parts of Vancouver Island. Then a lake, and when in the mountains I would almost give that the primary place and then a river.

Think of the millions of poor souls who spend their lives in the plains or in the great cities.

If I ever marry — and now it seems that unless this branch of our noble family is to die out I shall have to do so — I shall build a house on some promontory overlooking a bay and here I shall live.

The sea in the summer is a pleasant enough place but to waste one's life on it is a foolish thing. Man is not a fish. He is essentially a beast of the shore.

I should much like to see Helen's children. I hope they will grow up in her likeness. I have always considered Helen a woman of marked personality and a charm that is all her own.

Yours,
Fritz

In the following letter, Fritz again makes clear his preference for the spelling of his first name as 'Frederic' rather than 'Frederick'. Over the years, the Canadian government and other authorities have assumed the spelling should have a 'k' at the end.

My Dear Mother,

Very glad to get your letter and to hear that the young chee-ild has been christened Frederic without a "k" — a most important point and one which will doubtless have heavy bearing on the distinguished future that lies before him.

Glad to hear that Noel has got over at last. I will of course do anything I can for him. I have temporarily mislaid his address — a weakness of mine — please send it. The idea that I should take no notice of him is strongly distasteful to me. Poor Noel — if he is half-witted, it is no fault of his own.

I suppose you will be seeing old Father again soon. I should very much like to get hold of his political views on many subjects but I fear I never shall. Father is really pretty old now — old in mind. I don't think he troubles himself very much about past matters. Things today which may interest me enormously are to him things dead. And that indeed is I should imagine the case with very many men.

I am very glad that Helen married a Canadian and not an Englishman. I am a tremendous believer in country.

Heavens, the future that lies before this empire of ours is vast, enormous, tremendous in all its possibilities.

The 3rd great battle of Ypres is beginning — it is the biggest effort yet made. I see the flood of battle breaks again on St. Julien. This time, though, we are advancing. The initiative is with us.

Well, Mother, our personal losses have been pretty heavy, but upon my soul there are worse things than death. Jack and Gerald have died gloriously on the field of the battle for the Empire.

Just consider for a moment what the countries invaded go through. What it means to have home pillaged, the inmates shot or carried off. The terrible uncertainty as to what may have happened to those taken away. Our family losses are just one in many hundreds of thousands. Death is nothing compared to dishonour.

I wish you had something to interest yourself in. If you can think of anything which would at all interest you I wish you would let me know and I will get the matter up for you.

Life here is much as usual, which means that there is nothing to say and I am heartily bored with life in general.
My love to all.

Yours affectionately,
Fritz

DRAMATIC RESCUE OF Q SHIP SURVIVORS

Fritz's rescues while in command of the destroyer HMS *Christopher* included Capt. Gordon Campbell, VC, DSO and two bars, and his crew on HMS *Dunraven* in August 1917. *Dunraven* was a Q ship outfitted to appear as a lone merchant ship that a submarine would likely choose to sink with its surface artillery rather than wasting a valuable torpedo. The Q ships would wait until the sub surfaced and then unveil their own gunnery against it. The *Dunraven* had a classic confrontation with a sub which involved three faked evacuations, each time revealing a new hidden gun. Two Victoria Crosses were awarded in the episode.[2]

Campbell had won a Victoria Cross earlier in 1917 in Q ship action and could well have earned a bar to the VC with *Dunraven* but preferred to have two VCs go to his crew members in a ballot process. This personal modesty and sharing of honours with crew would have appealed to Fritz, but he likely disapproved of Q ships in principle because they involved disguises and deception rather than straight-up battle.

ATTEMPTS TO CONTACT GERALD IN THE AFTERLIFE

As was common with many distressed relations who lost loved ones in the Great War, Bertha tried spiritualism as a way to contact Gerald in the afterlife. Fritz, however, strongly disapproved of Bertha's participation in séances. In the following letter, he criticizes her for pursuing spiritualism and grieving excessively which demonstrated weakness at a time when maximum dedication was needed to defeat the enemy. He urges her to seek solace through the family's adherence to the Anglican Church.

This letter has the first of several complaints that brother Noel, finally overseas serving in Britain with the Canadian Forestry Corps, was remiss in not contacting him. It appears Noel was intimidated by his older brother who meant well but tended to dominate other family members with his forceful and decisive manner.

My Dear Mother,

Many thanks for your letter containing Noel's address, which I was very glad to get. Why on earth he didn't write me on coming to England I simply cannot conceive. However I have written him and hope I shall get news of him shortly.

Until further notice, please address my letters c/o Admiralty, White-hall, London, SWI.

Yes, Mother, I am afraid you have a heavy cross to bear. Yours is a loss which nothing can now replace, but remember you are one case in many, many thousands. Therefore to the outer world be determined to show a cheerful face and thereby keep your own self-respect. To me, of course, or to Helen say what you like. Remember things might be ever so much worse. Pick up the daily paper and look at the criminal courts and think of the misery brought into some family or other. Our boys have died an honourable death.

Look at Japan, study for a moment their customs. The man goes forth and dies in battle and the woman rejoices because he has so died. That is the only way to regard it — at any rate, in public.

And what good, anyhow, to dwell in your mind on this loss. You say you cannot help it. To a large degree this is true, but if you really make up your mind to it, it must go a long way towards it.

You talk, Mother, in your letters a great deal about spiritualism. I really question if it is a good thing. I do not pretend to have gone deeply into these matters, but anyhow it is a question about which little is known and much morbid nonsense written.

Your own consolation must lie in true religion. If you cannot believe in a future life, then indeed you are to be pitied, but if you do — then what need to give way to dejection, to steep yourself in misery. Heavens, Mother, the shortness of this life of ours. Surely while we are here, we can take our troubles, our losses in the right spirit, knowing them only to be just for such a little while.

You may count, Mother, on another score of years. It rests with you what you are going to make of them. Not only for yourself, but also for others and remember you owe a duty to others.

Don't tell me that in private you can allow your thoughts to dwell on these things and in public you can, as it were, anoint your face and assume a cheerful aspect because the thing is impossible; it simply cannot be done. No, you must firmly put these thoughts behind you and simply determine to infuse cheerfulness into this last twenty years of your life. It will not be an easy thing to do . . . There is only one thing that will enable you to do it, a firm and true belief in God and in an afterlife wherein we will all be united.

Remember. Mother, there are many things the human reason cannot cope with. Hold a stone in your hand, drop it, it falls and why? . . .

[rest of letter missing]

Here Fritz suggests to sister Helen that she support his efforts to discourage their mother from spiritualism and excessive grieving over Gerald's death.

FRITZ TO HIS SISTER HELEN   NOVEMBER 11, 1917

My diegle Hagen:

Ever so many thanks for your letter. Also for the photograph of the young boy Frederic.

I am really rather vague as to what a Godfather ought to do in these matters. A christening bowl or something like that appears to be indicated. A bit late in the day perhaps, but, then, the child will not remember. A bowl I believe in these affairs is the latest thing — a bowl therefore it will have to be.

For the moment I have not your letter by me and am certainly far too lazy to go up and get it. Besides, anyone who asks questions is a fool for they are seldom answered.

I have lately had a letter from Mother giving me Noel's address. It is a thing I find hard to explain why she should not have sent me it before. Noel has been over some time by now and it is only today, thanks to this delay, that I have written to him. Why on earth the boy didn't write me on his arrival I don't know. Mother writes a very miserable letter. I wish one could do something to get her out of this road on which her thoughts are always travelling. First of all, she seems keen on spiritualism. I do not pretend to have gone deeply into the matter but this I do know, there is little really known about spiritualism and there is a great deal of morbid nonsense written about it. It is just the last thing that Mother should dwell on or think she is going to get in touch with Gerald which is, of course, her ultimate object.

Mother has under normal circumstances another score of years on this world and it remains with her what use she is going to put them to. It is absolutely wrong of her to brood in her own mind on her loss. I do not say for a moment that she can banish the thought, but I am quite certain she can go a long way towards it, if she will but resolutely do her best to dismiss it on its entrance. If she can't do it alone, then you are the only person who can help her towards it. When the war is over I will see that she comes to England and I hope you will be able to come too.

The only real thing that can help Mother now is true religion and a firm belief in an afterlife and in God. Without these she is indeed to be pitied, but with them, what is the short wait on this earth. I am certain too that much real happiness awaits Mother if she will make up her mind to grasp it. Happiness in your family, and it is absolutely wrong for her to think that she has no happiness left in life itself, for be certain that, if she so thinks, she will never find it.

Many people have a harder cross to bear. Many people have had as heavy and worse losses. What is going to become of the Empire if everyone of them is going to remain hidden by their cloak of misery for the remainder of their days? It is morally wrong and Mother has got to so see it, or there is no future for her.

The war is likely to last a long time yet. Russia and now Italy have added to the years. The Hun is not yet beaten and will not be until we have driven him out of Belgium . . .

[rest of letter missing]

FRITZ'S UNCLE ARTHUR GRAY INJURED IN HALIFAX EXPLOSION

The Halifax Explosion on December 6, 1917 was the world's largest accidental man-made explosion, resulting from the collision of the French munitions ship *Mont Blanc* and the Norwegian freighter *Imo*. The blast seriously injured Bertha's stepbrother Arthur Cavendish Hamilton Gray, and destroyed many of the Gray family heirlooms that he inherited as John Hamilton Gray's only son.[3] Arthur, a veteran of the Boer War with the New Brunswick Regiment, was taken to England for treatment after the explosion and died there several years later.

There was little war-related spending in the safe Pacific port of Prince Rupert during the war, so the city's financial problems continued. Fred Peters continued his stressful work to keep the city from bankruptcy, to the point it affected his health. As an expert public speaker with strong opinions in support of the war effort, Fred was also regularly called on to speak at service club meetings and other community events. Among these, the *Prince Rupert News* covered his address on the history of the Royal Navy presented at the annual reunion in January 1918 of the veterans of the Battle of Paardeberg in the Boer War.[4]

In the following letter, Fritz asks his father for details of the family's financial position, as he was concerned about support for Bertha and Noel after Frederick's death. He also expresses interest in researching the family history, including the Peters crest.

My Dear Father,

I have been meaning for some time to write you on this matter — the question of our financial position. I hope you will not mind my asking, but there are several points which I should very much like to know.

First, what will be the exact position of affairs when you die? Second, what provision have you made for Mother and Noel? If I die, an insurance policy will cover my own debts and in the end, i.e. when the Admiralty pay out prize money, I suppose my next of kin would get some £300 or £400, certainly not more and probably less.

The question I particularly would like to know is about Mother. Her support would of course devolve on me, as also Noel, and I would very much like to know if you are going to leave anything towards it.

At the moment I am very heavily in debt. I always am in this perishing Navy. If I can get clear of debt — i.e. about £400 — I could allow Mother £120 while I am actually in command as I get about this much additional to my pay of 12/ a day. The war looks a long way from being finished, and after it I shall have no choice but to leave again and try and collect a few of these so deuced elusive dollars. It is quite hopeless to think of staying in the Navy if our present position financially is what I imagine it to be and marriage is equally out of the question which is I think a pity as our branch will thus die out. I suppose our family has not done much still it is a really Canadian family and I would very much like to see it continue. It is a pity that both the two boys have been killed.

I have never been told so but I imagine that Ted thinks he would have to contribute towards Mother's upkeep if you died — a thing I would not allow for a moment unless I found it impossible to do so myself. Anyhow I shall feel very much easier in my mind if it would not be too much trouble for you to let me know the whole state of affairs. Please do not forget to send me birth certificate. I wonder if you were able to raise me that two hundred I asked you for.

I would very much like to have what details you know concerning our family. Also the original of crest.

Yours as ever,
F.T.P.

Bertha's sisters Mim in Montreal and Florence in Guildford also participated in spiritualism, taking care to do it quietly to avoid antagonizing their children. One medium Bertha hired gave as a reference Sir Arthur Conan Doyle — the British physician best known as author of Sherlock Holmes books. After his mother's death in 1906 and subsequent deaths of other relations, Conan Doyle found solace in Spiritualism and existence beyond the grave.

Bertha wrote to Conan Doyle at his estate in East Sussex complaining about the medium. Conan Doyle described Annie Brittain as an "excellent medium" in his book *The History of Spiritualism*. He often referred mourning relatives to her in the war, noting the example of a suicidal widow who was heartened by her work. He greatly regretted that Annie was arrested and hauled into police court, saying the incident showed they were in a "dark age" in world history.

It is possible Bertha's main motivation for the letter was the thrill of corresponding with the famous writer.

SIR ARTHUR CONAN DOYLE TO BERTHA   NOVEMBER 23, 1917

Crowborough

Dear Mrs. Peters,

I have all sympathy that can be of little help. I don't understand it. I know Mrs. Brittain's powers and I have found her very reliable, so should be inclined to back her opinion.

Yours sincerely,
A. Conan Doyle

BRITISH DISTINGUISHED SERVICE CROSS

In March 1918, Fritz received the Distinguished Service Cross medal — the third-level British honour for valour — from King George V for "showing exceptional initiative, ability and zeal in submarine hunting operations and complete disregard of danger, exceptional coolness and ingenuity in his attacks on enemy submarines," according to the citation. Although he experienced more than his fair share of battle at sea, he still complained in his letters home of the long periods of boredom between engagements. Nowhere in the letters does he indicate any fear of injury or death in battle.

After years of expecting a quick Allied victory in the war, when it finally happened in the fall of 1918, it came as a surprise to Fritz who expected further fighting in 1919 and beyond. In the following letter, he reflects on how the Great War would be remembered in history. He mentions a visit to Gerald's grave, but a temporary gravesite with marker was subsequently destroyed by shelling as ground changed hands in the war. With the war over, he expects to be able to get away for leaves. One of the downsides of peace was reduced pay.

CHAPTER SEVEN

1918 – 1939
QUEST FOR LIVELIHOOD AND ADVENTURE BETWEEN WARS

Firstly, you must always implicitly obey orders, without attempting to form any opinion of your own regarding their propriety. Secondly, you must consider every man your enemy who speaks ill of your King; and thirdly you must hate a Frenchman as you hate the devil.

— Admiral Nelson, advice to a midshipman, 1793

FRITZ TO HIS MOTHER BERTHA   NOVEMBER 18, 1918

My Dear Mother,

So the end is reached. I wish it were a happier end for you.

I am not sure of my movements. I suppose the fleet will not be demobilized for some months to come. When it is I shall apply for half pay.

I am going to take the first opportunity of going over to see about Gerald's grave.

As soon as I can arrange it I will get you over but I do not expect to be able to do so for a year or so after I leave the Navy as I shall not be able to afford it before then.

I do not advise, either, that you come over for at least a year, and I would suggest that Helen should come over as well.

Well, it has been a very great page in history. A hundred years hence how very bored very many people will be with it and the thousand books on it and theories and Lord knows what.

I only hope that the Huns responsible for the ill treatment of our prisoners get their full deserts. I should have liked to have seen Germany suffer something that Belgium has suffered.

Pity the Hun fleet did not come out, thereby spoiling the one good show the Navy might have had. Yes, a great pity. Would have done our Navy a world of good and repaid them something for four and a half years of unutterable boredom, but it was not to be.

Well, I should not be so very surprised to see myself in Canada before next year is out.

Yours affectionately,
Fritz

P.S. Very many thanks for the chocolates which made a belated arrival, but which were none the less excellent.

Fritz and his father were probably proud of the contribution of Cunard ships to the war effort. Liners seconded for war duties transported 900,000 soldiers across the Atlantic, along with seven million tons of food and war supplies.[1] This achievement came at a high price, however, as German U-boats sank about half of the Cunard fleet.

Five months later, demobilization of Allied military personnel was far from complete. With the war over, Fritz complained more than ever about boredom at sea. He expresses concern that the radicalism of the Russian Revolution would spread elsewhere in the world. The photograph he mentions is of a memorial in St. Peter's Church in Charlottetown with the names of Jack Peters, Gerald Peters and a cousin, Sergeant-Major Arthur Gordon Peters, son of Fred's brother Arthur, who served with U.S. forces and died in 1918.

FRITZ TO HIS MOTHER BERTHA   APRIL 2, 1919

Dear Mother:

I have received your letter of March 5th and will accordingly make the arrangements about Gerald's grave. I will also arrange the tablet in St. Peter's Cathedral in Charlottetown and will have the same photographed and sent to you. I would like the date and place when Jack went missing and the same when Gerald was killed.

I haven't heard whether Noel has left or not as he has not written since telling me (last January) that he was sailing next week. I presume he has left.

Sorry to hear Father is so unwell, and hope this will find him better.

I will have my photo done when next I am in London tho' it seems a waste of time and money and I am sure it can do the camera no good.

Not much news from here. Life is very dull and desperately boring with nothing to do. Summer, thank heaven, will shortly be with us. It has been pretty chilly here lately.

Very little news. I hope that Bolshevism is not going to envelop everything.

> Yours,
> *Fritz.*

The Royal Navy in a new era of peace was expected to radically downsize, but they didn't want to lose Fritz Peters. He was selected for the first Staff College after the war at the Royal Naval College. In March 1920, Fritz was promoted to lieutenant commander and assigned to the Commander-in-Chief Atlantic Fleet as war staff officer on the battleship HMS *Queen Elizabeth*, but he decided to retire in June 1920 and return to civilian life.

The prospect of peacetime service did not appeal to him. Through his naval career, he preferred serving on action-oriented smaller vessels like destroyers rather than the much larger cruisers and battleships which tended to be more formal and bureaucratic and see less action. He also hoped he could overcome his never-ending problems with debt by making more money as a civilian.

END OF THE LINE FOR FATHER IN PRINCE RUPERT

Fred Peters continued working for the city of Prince Rupert almost until his death at 69 on July 29, 1919, two weeks after his sister Carrie Bayfield died in Vancouver.[2] Carrie Peters and her husband Ned Bayfield had moved west in retirement to Vancouver, as suggested by their son Francis Bayfield, who became a successful lawyer and magistrate in Vancouver after articling with the Tupper-Peters law firm in Victoria.

Fred had been in declining health since the spring, but he managed to travel to New Denver to visit Bertha and his daughter Helen's family. He died alone, a tragic figure depressed by the disappointments of his career, and still grieving the loss of two sons in the war. The story in the family was that he died of a broken heart. His was a career poised for greatness, but thwarted by near misses, well-intentioned miscalculations and a changing world that passed him by and decimated his family. As Fritz noted in a letter to his mother, his father was "truly a might-have-been". He dedicated the last eight years of his life to keeping Prince Rupert from bankruptcy. In an editorial, the *Prince Rupert Daily News* said "he was more than a public servant, he was an institution".[3]

BURIAL AT ROSS BAY CEMETERY

Fritz got leave to return to British Columbia to organize his father's funeral. As directed in his father's will, the funeral was in Victoria and burial at historic Ross Bay Cemetery beside the small stone marking the grave of daughter Violet who died in 1905. Plates were attached to two sides of his tombstone to commemorate sons Gerald and Jack who died in the war.

JOBS IN CANADA SCARCE FOR VETERANS

By the time of Fritz's second resignation from the navy, most other B.C. veterans had returned to the province and jobs were scarce. His whereabouts during the inter-war years have long been a mystery. Reports from friends and colleagues indicate he returned to Canada for a short time and was involved in strange business ventures such as selling boots to Russians. Considering his disdain for communism, this may have involved supplying the anti-Bolshevik forces in the conflicts after the Russian Revolution.

The people he turned to in looking for a new career were his friends from navy service. One of these was Paymaster-Commander Saxton, who became a lawyer and held the position of Managing Director of the Gold Coast Political Service in the colony in west-central Africa now known as Ghana.[4] With his friend Saxton as a valuable contact, Fritz went to Gold Coast and was hired to work for a company involved in international commerce where he willingly started at the bottom as a clerk and worked his way up. For Fritz, the undeveloped Gold Coast, with potential opportunities in a frontier environment, may have appealed in similar fashion to how Canada's Yukon and West Coast appealed to his father two decades earlier.

FOILING HIT MEN ON AFRICA'S GOLD COAST

Fritz moved from this work to growing cocoa at a Gold Coast plantation. While farming may seem an unlikely occupation for a man of action like Fritz, it came with significant hazards in the unruly frontier environment. Saxton told a London columnist in 1943 that there were at least three attempts on Fritz's life, one where a car tried to run him over on the side of a road. Then in a second attack, a man tried to smash him in the head with a wrench. He also found a poisonous Mamba snake in his bed one night. Saxton said in each case Fritz "took care" of his assailants.[5]

In Kumasi, Gold Coast, in about 1930, are, from left: Paymaster-Commander (Ret.) Sydney W. 'Swain' Saxton, RN; Capt. (Ret.) Harry Dunbar-Rivers, RN; Lt-Cdr (Ret.) F.T. Peters, DSO, DSC, RN.

DEFENDING ROYAL NAVY HONOUR

Saxton also recalled a dinner party in Gold Coast where a loud large man looked at Fritz and said contemptuously, "You may have your DSO and you may have command of the ships, but what the hell is the Royal Navy doing today?" Fritz took no notice of the unpleasant fellow, but after dinner went to him and said, "You insulted me at dinner. I don't mind that, but you also insulted the service to which I am proud to belong. Now I am going to knock hell out of you." Fritz then proceeded to knock the man down.[6]

Saxton encouraged Fritz to become a fellow lawyer as, with several relatives and friends established as lawyers, entering the profession would have been "an easy ball at his feet". He offered to lend Fritz money to pay for law school, but Fritz declined because he doubted he would be able to pay Saxton back. Fritz knew he shared his parents' inability to live within his means.

Some of Fritz's friends noticed a pattern with Fritz in the twenties and thirties. He would go to Gold Coast for two or three years to make money, and then come back to England for enjoyable reunions with his navy buddies, returning to Africa when his money ran out. Restless by nature, he realized that it was doubtful that he would ever marry and settle down. Instead, he became an unofficial member of the families of his navy buddies — particularly Swain Saxton and Cromwell Varley.

MIDGET SUBMARINE DEVELOPMENT

Retired commander Varley — who, like Fritz, won a Distinguished Service Order medal in the First World War — was the inventor of midget submarines that the Royal Navy used occasionally in the Second World War. Variations of the tiny subs were made in one-man, two-man and three-man sizes. The base in the Clyde in Scotland for the midget subs was called Varbel, after Varley and his partner Bell. Fritz helped with the project by designing and building the pumps for the mini-subs,[7] possibly at the engineering works near Bristol that he mentions in a 1942 letter. As there are no records of Fritz in engineering school or being trained as an engineer, his involvement with an engineering works and assisting in the development of midget subs are among the mysteries of Fritz's life.

Fritz Peters in about 1935.

Commander Joel wrote in the 1950s that he lost touch with Fritz in the time between the wars, aside from the midget sub work with Varley. "I gathered that he tended to wander over the face of the Earth, settling nowhere and I think not achieving much. I believe he was for some time in Canada. But wherever he was, I am sure he made many friends," Joel said.

Saxton, Varley and Joel would likely agree that a key reason for the gaps in information about Fritz's life was his excessive modesty. He loved telling stories about the Empire and the Navy, but not about himself. In his mind, such talk was unseemly and bordered on American-style boasting.

BERTHA MOVES WITH HELEN'S FAMILY

Back in B.C., Bertha Peters brought along her cherished books and P.E.I. furniture each time her son-in-law was transferred to a new West Kootenay community. They moved to Rossland in 1920, nearby Trail in 1927 and Nelson in 1929. She helped with the children and had exceptional cooking skills from her days in P.E.I., though her insistence on perfection and her anguish when problems arose made some mealtimes unpleasant for the Dewdney family. Like Fritz at sea, Bertha, Helen and Ted were all ardent bridge players. Bertha rated each community in the region by the quality of its bridge players.[8]

Ted never complained about his mother-in-law staying with the family. He probably sympathized with her for the loss of two boys in the war, and felt uncomfortable being safe in B.C. while his brothers-in-law were in the thick of the fighting.

Helen was popular in each community they moved to because of her success in organizing and performing in music and theatre productions using local amateur talent. She was also a remarkably good conciliator. If two people among her acquaintances were feuding, she would invite them both to tea and all would leave as friends.

Politics and current events were regular topics of conversation at the Dewdney dinner table. A big change for everyone after the war was Canadian women being able to vote in elections for the first time. Ted, strongly influenced as a boy by his Conservative uncle Edgar, found himself outnumbered by the two Liberal ladies in the house when they travelled together by horse and buggy to the polling station on election day.

BERTHA CRIPPLED BY FALL

Bertha was in good health until a serious fall down the stairs of the Nelson house in about 1935 prevented her from ever walking again. Still, her grandchildren were amazed at her undiminished mind and remarkable skill in solving crossword puzzles. Even as a bedridden invalid in her eighties, she regularly won cash prizes for puzzle contests sponsored by newspapers.

A regular visitor at the Dewdney house in Nelson in the 1930s was son Peter Dewdney's best friend and fishing buddy Robert Hampton 'Hammy' Gray, who would earn a posthumous Victoria Cross for a daring attack that sank a Japanese warship just days before the end of World War Two. During his visits to the Dewdney house Hammy dutifully paid his respects to Mrs. Peters, often asking about her son Fritz who distinguished himself with the Royal Navy in the Great War.

While communication between Fritz and his family was scarce in this period, he was pleased to hear his niece Eve Dewdney was to marry Sandon, B.C.-born mining engineer Jack Fingland in October 1933, sending a gold watch as a wedding gift. When Helen was finally able to contact Fritz with letters in early 1942, it was the first he had heard of Eve's children born in 1936 and 1938.

In 1943, Fritz's cousin William Hamilton Abbott was quoted in a *Montreal Gazette* article saying Fritz was involved in British secret intelligence work in the years between the wars. It would not be a surprise to learn that he had substantial field experience in British intelligence before his appointment as commander of the Brickendonbury spy school in 1940.

CHAPTER EIGHT

1939 – 1940
ATTACKING SUBS FROM TRAWLERS

Once more unto the breach, dear friends, once more;
Or close the wall up with our English dead.
. . .Follow your spirit; and upon this charge
Cry "God for Harry, England and St. George!"

— "King Henry V" by William Shakespeare

With war between Britain and Germany clearly on the horizon in August 1939, Fritz worked his way from Africa back to England on a freighter to rejoin the Royal Navy. While several contemporaries from cadet days and the First World War were rejected because of age, Fritz, with his stellar record in the Great War, was welcomed back for his third stint with the navy.

In October 1939, he took command of a group of anti-submarine trawlers that included his ship HMS *Stanhope*, a five-year-old fishing trawler adapted with depth charge racks, ASDIC sound detection and gunnery. For someone who relished commanding the newest class of speedy destroyers in the First War, Fritz had to swallow his pride to command these converted fishing vessels, but he made the best of it and focused on doing the job. The following January he took command of the trawler HMS *Thirlmere* and the 10th Anti-Submarine Strike Force.[1] Operating in the Orkneys and Shetland command, the force sank two subs, and Fritz won his second British Distinguished Service Cross. In line with military tradition, he was given a bar to add to his DSC medal won in the First World War.

NO PATIENCE FOR THE TERROR OF TOBERMORY

Fritz was keen on inventions like plastic explosives and Varley's tiny submarines, but resistant to change in other areas. Commander Joel said he encountered Fritz at the navy base of Greenock, Scotland, when Fritz was in command of an anti-aircraft frigate, an assignment he didn't enjoy because, like Joel, Fritz wasn't much interested in 'flying machines'. Fritz was soon back to his specialty — fighting submarines.

Joel also told the story of Fritz being sent for training at Tobermory off the west coast of Scotland under Admiral Sir Gilbert 'Puggie' Stephenson. Known as the Terror of Tobermory, Stephenson had a reputation for strict efficiency and giving hell to trainees. Fritz took his ship in for the training, but was soon put off by Stephenson's antics and sailed away without doing the program, earning renown in the navy as the only man to defy Puggie.[2]

Fritz with wife of his close friend Swain Saxton.

Fritz was in the naval battles at Narvik on the west coast of Norway in April 1940. In a conversation in 1943 with a London newspaper columnist, his friend Saxton recalled encountering Fritz on his return from Narvik and hearing him say: "Forget all you saw or heard in the last war. This is hell, but I still have my sword sharpened. Perhaps someday I shall be able to board and use it."[3]

TRAGIC ATTACK ON FORMER ALLY

After the fall of France in June 1940, British Prime Minister Winston Churchill put top priority on ensuring the large French navy did not fall into the hands of the Nazis. The new French government based in Vichy promised it would scuttle its ships before allowing them to be taken over, but Churchill gave no value to a pledge from a government beholden to the Nazis. In a coordinated effort at locations around the world, British forces on July 3, 1940, took control of French ships or confronted their commanders with demands that they be neutralized and safe from German takeover. Churchill was particularly concerned about the French warships in the naval base of Mers-el-Kebir on the west side of Oran Bay, a couple of miles from the city of Oran in western Algeria. He sent a task force under Vice Admiral Sir James Somerville to demand the French accept one of several choices for neutralizing their ships moored at the base.

Somerville sent Fritz's buddy from China Station days, Capt. Hook Holland, the French-speaking commander of the carrier HMS *Ark Royal* who had served as naval attaché in Paris, to present a list of options to French Admiral Marcel-Bruno Gensoul. To the deep regret of Somerville, Holland and many others in the Royal Navy task force, Gensoul, who resented negotiating with an officer of lower rank, did not agree to any of the options by the deadline. Led by battleship HMS *Hood*, the task force set its heavy guns on the base, quickly destroying most of the ships and killing 1,297 French sailors. French of all stripes were furious at Britain for taking this action, but it was loudly applauded in Britain and by U.S. President Roosevelt, who saw it as proof that the British were determined to fight on against the Nazis. The Vichy government responded by breaking relations with Britain and launching a token attack on the British base at Gibraltar. Fritz had no part in the Mers-el-Kebir destruction, but the resulting anti-British rage would have an impact on his mission in the other Oran harbour 28 months later.

CHAPTER NINE

1940 – 1941
COMMANDING A SCHOOL FOR SPIES

It takes three years to build a ship;
it takes three centuries to build a tradition.

— Admiral Sir Andrew Browne Cunningham, Crete, 1941

In June 1940, Fritz was seconded to be commandant of a British Secret Intelligence Service (SIS) school for training spies and saboteurs for anti-Nazi operations in Occupied Europe. It was part of Churchill's scheme to "set Europe ablaze" with attacks from within Axis-controlled countries. At that point in the war, with no indication that either the United States or Russia would join the fight against the Nazis, Churchill looked to such revolts as just about the only hope for winning the war.

The spy school was set up as Station XVIII at Brickendonbury Hall, a large country home and former school near Hertford. Fritz's colleagues at the school included Guy Burgess and Kim Philby, who years later were revealed to have been Soviet spies since their days at Cambridge University in the 1930s. The school was established by Burgess and Monty Chidson, deputy head of Section D (for destruction) of SIS. Section D had a key role in the development of plastic explosives and time delay fuses, and offered a special industrial demolition course at Brickendonbury. Most of the students in the school were expatriates from occupied countries who later returned to fight the Germans from within.

Philby, who came to SIS after working as a war correspondent for the *Times of London*, was in charge of instruction of propagandists. Among the other instructors at Brickendonbury were the Russian-speaking operative George Hill, art dealer Tommy Harris, an explosives expert named Clark, and two former Shanghai police officers who were experts in the art of silent killing and unarmed combat. One of Philby's ideas for upsetting the Germans was to spread the rumour in the Continent that French women with venereal diseases were intentionally luring German soldiers to infect them.[1]

GENTLE SMILE OF GREAT CHARM

Despite their political differences, the Communist Philby liked and admired Commander Peters, preferring him to other higher-ups in the intelligence service who tended to be bland businessmen. Philby described Fritz in his memoirs as having "faraway naval eyes and a gentle smile of great charm". He was surprised that Fritz got along well with Guy Burgess, who most people found obnoxious, and was constantly helping himself to Fritz's supply of cigarettes. Fritz took Burgess and Philby to dinner several times at the Hungaria, one of his favourite restaurants in the Soho area of London, to listen to their ideas on projects.[2]

Philby recalled one day at Brickendonbury when the students were shouting in an assortment of languages about parachutists landing in the yard outside the school. Fritz, in bed suffering from eczema, said he doubted such an attack was possible. "If the Germans have invaded, I shall get up," Fritz said calmly. "I don't know what I shall do if I do get up, but I shall certainly take command." He ordered some Belgians to put on their uniforms and man a gun overlooking the yard. It turned out to be just a mine on a parachute, so Fritz's scepticism was justified. His insistence that the Belgians fight in uniform demonstrated his personal sense of honour in battle, even when it may have cost time in fighting off an enemy.

BUREAUCRACY AND TURF BATTLE BOTHERED PETERS

In these early days of Special Operations, the jurisdictions for intelligence work overlapped across several agencies and ministries, and Fritz found himself in the middle of bureaucratic infighting. Philby said he noticed that Fritz looked troubled. "As the summer weeks went by without any clear direction from London, the commander's aspect changed for the worse. He became more than usually taciturn and withdrawn."

"He fell into a deep depression," Philby noted. "It was no surprise when he summoned Guy and myself one morning and told us he had spent the previous night composing his resignation. He spoke sadly, as if conscious of failure and neglect. Then he cheered up and the charming smile came back, for the first time in many days. He was clearly happy to be going back to his little ships after his brief baptism of political fire." [3]

TRAINEES ADORED THEIR COMMANDER

Philby noted that Peters was later awarded a posthumous Victoria Cross "for what was probably unnecessarily gallant behaviour in Oran harbour. When I heard of the award, I felt a pang that he would never have known about it. He was the type of strong sentimentalist who would have wept at such honour. Our trainees came to adore him."

In February 1941, Fritz began working with the Director of Anti-Submarine Warfare in naval intelligence and in April was appointed Staff Officer (Operations) to the Commander in Chief, Portsmouth. In August 1941, he was made Acting Captain and put in command of HMS *Tynewald*, an auxiliary anti-aircraft cruiser, beginning a year with the ship that included a tour of duty in Far Eastern waters.

A few months after Fritz's resignation at the school, Section D separated from the SIS and became part of the new Special Operations Executive. In 1942, the SOE would assist Fritz in planning and preparations for a top secret, extremely hazardous mission in what was then the largest amphibious invasion in history.

Chapter Ten

August – October 1942
Smack in the Middle of U.S. – British Hostility

There is only one thing worse than fighting with allies,
and that is fighting without them.

— Winston S. Churchill

The following letter is particularly valuable in telling Fritz's story because it is the only letter in the Peters Family Papers from the Second World War era. Fritz's sister Helen and her family in Nelson, B.C., made several inquiries trying to contact him after losing touch with Fritz in the 1930s. Despite a small population of about 7,000, Nelson was a regional centre with a cosmopolitan flair. Its mines, orchards and idyllic setting on Kootenay Lake surrounded by the Selkirk Range mountains attracted a diverse mix of residents, including several English widows who became Bertha's close friends. Helen's daughter Eve spent most of the war in New York where her husband Jack worked as an inspector and administrator with the massive industrial war mobilization program.

Some of Bertha's friends continued to visit her at the house after she was crippled by a fall in the mid-1930s, but her main companion and caregiver was her granddaughter Rose Pamela 'Dee Dee' Dewdney, the only child remaining in the home after her brother Peter went to university in Alberta. Dee Dee was extremely curious about the mysterious Uncle Fritz she had never met.

As noted in his letter, Fritz was thrilled with the success just days earlier of the British raid on the huge Normandie dry dock at St. Nazaire on France's Atlantic coast. When commandos destroyed the dock, the only repair facilities for the largest German ships such as *Tirpitz* were in home waters in the Baltic. The raid involved directing an old destroyer full of explosives towards the port facilities and setting off the explosion on time delay to make lasting damage.

FRITZ TO HIS SISTER HELEN   MARCH 31, 1942

United Service Club, Pall Mall
My dearest Helen

I was so pleased to get your letter of 30th January which reached me a few days ago. I was most interested to hear about children and to realize that I am now a great uncle. Eve seems to have had a very interesting time and I should imagine her husband is kept pretty busy at the moment. I was very interested to hear that Peter is now a sub[i]. I wonder where he will fetch up. I must say it looks like a long grim business and God only knows when it will end. Still so much that was unexpected has already happened that perhaps the end when it comes will arrive with startling suddenness. How is Mother? Poor Mother, I have grieved so much for her misfortunes. She has had much unhappiness and pain. And what has happened to Noel?

About myself I can indeed give you little news. Censorship stops me saying anything about my present job. What I shall do after the war I do not know. I was formerly running an engineering works — since bombed out. If I can work it in, I will pay you a visit after the war whenever that may be and if one is still in the land of the living. Aunt Helen[ii] is very old . . . I saw her last July. Her mind is still active and alive when she is all right. Some people living next door to her look in pretty often and I correspond pretty regularly with them so that I am informed of what is going on. Aunt Helen does not write at all nowadays. I expect I shall see her this summer if I get leave. A fair number of bombs dropped round her neighbourhood which was a noisy one being only 10 or 12 miles from Bristol.

Aunt Annie is also still alive, I think she is 87. Her mind has nearly gone. The two of them are well looked after by a very good maid.

I never got off at Nelson so have no idea what it is like. It must be pleasant having a lake. I hope Ted is enjoying his retirement. Just at the present what I am looking forward to is some leave and some rest. I am beginning to feel my age.

This affair at St. Nazaire last week was most inspiring to hear of. Give my love to Dee and tell her one day I hope to see her. My love to you.

Fritz

i.   After training at HMCS *Royal Roads* on Vancouver Island, Frederic "Peter" Dewdney became a sub – lieutenant with the Royal Canadian Navy.

ii. Fred's cousin Helen Francklyn, and her sister Annie Francklyn, both spinster granddaughters of Sir Samuel Cunard.

Seven months later, Fritz would find himself in charge of an even riskier attack on an Algerian harbour. Instead of destruction, the goal of the mission — code-named Operation Reservist — was to keep the city of Oran's harbour intact for use in the Allied invasion of North Africa, known as Operation Torch, the first combined operation of the British and Americans and a turning point in the Second World War. Until the North Africa invasion — coinciding almost exactly with British Gen. Montgomery's victory at El Alamein in Egypt — the initiative in the war was always with the Germans.

BRITAIN WELCOMES A POWERFUL NEW ALLY

The United States entered the Second World War after the Japanese attack on their naval base at Pearl Harbor on December 7, 1941, almost two and a half years after Britain and France went to war against Germany. In Churchill's history of the war, he said he felt a great sense of relief when he heard of the Pearl Harbor attack because he knew it meant that Britain would eventually win the war with its new partner who would bring an enormous industrial base and military capability to support its war effort. Reflecting on the lowest points of the war to date, he included "the horrible episode at Oran" — referring to the Royal Navy's reluctant bombardment of French warships at the Mers-el-Kebir naval base on the western outskirts of Oran soon after France surrendered to Germany in 1940.[1]

For years, President Roosevelt wanted to help Britain against the Nazis, but his support was limited by a strong isolationist movement in the U.S. This obstacle was overcome when Hitler declared war on the U.S. on December 9, 1941, in line with his pact with Japan.

In the months after Pearl Harbor, the British and Americans went through a painful period of bickering on key aspects of war planning. Many Americans wanted to concentrate first on the Pacific region where they were attacked by the Japanese, but Churchill convinced Roosevelt that Germany was the greater threat and needed to be the first priority. Then the Americans, with a tradition of going straight at an enemy, commenced preparations for an invasion across the English Channel in 1942 to establish a beachhead to draw enemy forces away from the Eastern Front at a time when it appeared the Russians were close to surrender and desperately needed help.

The British, with their tradition of superior naval power, preferred to attack an enemy at its weak points on the periphery rather than head on. Churchill worried about the consequences of a disastrous premature invasion of Europe, and a protracted struggle in trenches similar to the First World War.

The concept of invading North Africa first came up at the Arcadia Conference between Churchill and Roosevelt in Washington shortly after America entered the war. On July 25, 1942, Roosevelt took the extraordinary step of overruling the unanimous opinion of his military advisors and agreed to an invasion of North Africa in 1942 rather than a cross-channel invasion. An angry Lt. Gen. Dwight D. 'Ike' Eisenhower, commander of American troops in England, said it was "the blackest day in history".[2] However, after the war Eisenhower admitted that the British were right to oppose an early invasion of Europe, mainly because German air strength at the time would have devastated any Allied bridgehead in France.

INVASIONS DESPERATELY NEEDED GOOD HARBOURS

A mission to capture Oran harbour was originally part of the plan for the North Africa invasion, then cancelled when it was thought the French got word of it, and finally reinstated because the Allies desperately needed good ports for landing huge numbers of tanks and other supplies for the invasion. It was estimated that between 600 and 700 tons of supplies per day were required for each landed division (about 15,000 troops) in North Africa.[3]

A key objective of the invaders was to move forces eastward as quickly as possible to Tunisia, the French colony directly south of Sicily, before the Germans had time to bring in reinforcements and build up their defences. Following up on Montgomery's victory at El Alamein in Egypt that concluded on November 5, 1942, the Allies wanted to clear Germans from Africa as soon as possible to secure sea lanes in the Mediterranean Sea and use North Africa as a base for attacking Continental Europe.

Eisenhower was appointed commander of the North Africa invasion, with both American and British subordinates reporting to him. He had virtually no combat experience but was valued for his organizational skills, political savvy and genial personality. For the invasion, he looked for advice on planning and tactics to his naval head and deputy commander, British Admiral Sir Andrew Cunningham, a veteran of extensive action against the Axis powers, including massive victories against the Italian navy. In a letter to U.S. Army Chief of Staff George Marshall, Eisenhower lavished praise on Cunningham: "His frankness, his generous and selfless attitude, his obvious determination and, above all, his direct action methods and impatience with ritual and red tape, all come as a refreshing breath of spring".[4] Fritz Peters' friends and admirers would say the same compliments applied to him as well. Like Fritz, Cunningham commanded destroyers and was highly decorated in the First World War, winning the Distinguished

Service Order and two bars, and known for an aggressive, attack-oriented approach to battle.

CUNNINGHAM APPOINTS FRITZ TO DUTIES IN OPERATION TORCH

In August 1942, Admiral Cunningham appointed Fritz as special operations and naval planner, working under the British chief naval planner, Admiral Bertram Ramsay. With Cunningham's backing and Fritz's service record, Fritz's offence-minded approach in organizing and carrying out an audacious harbour attack was not unexpected.

For the three-pronged attack on French North Africa, Eisenhower made the following appointments: U.S. Maj. Gen. Lloyd R. Fredendall to command the Centre Task Force of American and British forces to capture Oran; U.S. Maj. Gen. George Patton to command the all-U.S. Western Task Force to capture Casablanca, and; British Lt.-Gen. Kenneth Anderson to command the Eastern Task Force of British and Americans to capture Algiers. British Commodore Thomas Troubridge was Centre Task Force's naval commander, and U.S. Maj. Gen. James Doolittle, famous for leading the air attack on Tokyo in April 1942, was its air chief. No Canadian units were included in the North Africa landings. Had the Allies chosen the alternative of northern Norway for their first invasion rather than North Africa, Churchill planned extensive use of Canadian troops for cold weather fighting.

At this early stage of American involvement in the war, their commanders, officers and troops all suffered from inexperience. Ineffective commanders like Gen. Fredendall were not yet weeded out. Along with other faults, Fredendall was a notoriously bad communicator. Supposedly to increase security, he used a convoluted personal code for phone calls that no one could understand.[5] An extreme anglophobe, Fredendall encouraged his staff to mock their allies by talking with fake English accents. His incompetence and cowardice would be revealed later in the North African campaign. With his disdain for Americans, Fritz likely found his Centre Task Force head Fredendall particularly difficult to work with.

DYSFUNCTIONAL RELATIONSHIP BETWEEN ALLIES

The next subject of disagreement between the Brits and the Americans was the location of landing sites for Operation Torch. The British wanted to land as far east as possible, so as to reach Tunisia in central North Africa before the Germans. Disregarding British assurances, the Americans feared they could be trapped in the Mediterranean Sea region if the Axis nations

— with support from fascist but neutral Spain — were able to close the Strait of Gibraltar, so they pushed instead for an attack on Morocco on the Atlantic coast. The other attraction of the Morocco landings for the Americans was that they could do it on their own, without involvement or interference from the British.

These disagreements and other disputes contributed to tension and acrimony at meetings between the military leaders of the two nations. The British resented the Americans as Johnny-come-latelies who had stayed on the sidelines while Britain stood alone against the Nazis. American officers acknowledged the British had more experience, but pointed out that the Brits' experience amounted to nothing more than a succession of defeats. Royal Navy officers like Fritz were exasperated by the American reluctance to take their hard-learned advice on anti-sub warfare, such as the use of convoys and blacking out coastal cities. Americans were suspicious that Britain might use them to retain and expand the British Empire, which, as a former colony, Americans did not support.

As overall commander, Eisenhower did all he could to improve relations for the good of the alliance, such as issuing this order to American officers: "You can call a man a son of a bitch, but you can't call him a British son of a bitch."[6]

UNCERTAINTY ABOUT FRENCH REACTION

The biggest question mark was how the French would react to the invasion. Would the Allies be greeted as liberators or enemies? The peace settlement after Germany's conquest of France in 1940 split the country into Occupied France, under direct German control, and Vichy France — including French colonies — which was supposedly autonomous but had leaders beholden to the Nazis. To ensure the French complied with the terms of the peace settlement, the Nazis kept more than a million French soldiers as prisoners. They allowed the French to maintain military forces in their North Africa colonies to fend off attacks.

Many French — particularly expatriates living abroad in places like Oran — resigned themselves to supporting the Nazis because the alternative of communism was even more fearful. Others approved of the anti-Jewish laws enacted by the Vichy government, particularly the Arab peoples of French North Africa. Also, legality was important to the French, and the legal authority was the government at Vichy, to which officers were required to swear loyalty.

After the Royal Navy's capture and destruction of French warships in 1940 and conflicts with the British in distant French colonies like Madagascar and Dakar, many Frenchmen hated Britain more than

Germany. They also resented being included in Britain's naval blockade against Axis nations. In contrast to the bad relations between Britain and France, the United States in 1942 still had full diplomatic relations with Vichy France and a traditional friendship with France going back to the Revolutionary War. The chief U.S. diplomatic representative in North Africa, Robert Murphy, and his staff, nicknamed the Twelve Apostles, sought out French military leaders supportive of the Allied side to encourage a pro-Allied coup to coincide with the invasion, but had to be extremely careful not to disclose any hint of the upcoming landings because surprise was of utmost importance.

DISPUTE LEADS TO COMPROMISES

Eisenhower's delegation of authority for naval planning and operations to British Admiral Cunningham was not unexpected, as the British had more ships involved in the invasion than the Americans as well as extensive battle experience. However, this did not sit well with American officers, who resented serving under foreign command and found much to criticize in the plans put forward by the British.

Fritz's original plan was for the Oran harbour attack to begin "with all guns blazing" within 15 minutes of the landings of troops on beaches to the west and east of Oran.[7] However, because of the importance of keeping the harbour in good shape for the Allies, he was told not to fire first. There was heated opposition to the plan from the Americans, particularly U.S. Rear Admiral Andrew C. Bennett, who fretted that the harbour attack group would be annihilated if the French responded with full force.

The bitter exchanges in meetings led to Bennett writing an October 17, 1942, memo to Eisenhower saying he was concerned Capt. Peters would go ahead with a frontal assault on Oran harbour regardless of the progress of the landing forces on the beaches.[8] From Fritz's perspective, the condescending, obnoxious Americans had no business second-guessing the experience and expertise of the Royal Navy — still the largest and greatest navy in the world — regarding a naval operation.

Despite Bennett's warnings, Eisenhower continued to support the special mission to take over the harbours. In an October 29, 1942, letter to Gen. Marshall, Eisenhower said he expected the French navy would provide stronger resistance to the invasion than the French army, but once the navy saw the army collapse, they would likely follow suit and also surrender to the Allies. "At the very least, we should find divided councils among the French which should prevent them from offering really effective resistance," Eisenhower noted. Commenting on special action being taken to capture the two major ports, he said planners "have set up two small commando type of expeditions to enter Oran and Algiers very quickly after H-hour [the beach landings on the flanks of each city] so as to prevent sabotage and the blocking of harbours and piers".[9] As a compromise to alleviate American concerns, Cunningham decreed that Operation Reservist would tentatively start two hours after the first landing crafts arrived on beaches west and east of Oran, with the idea that by then Allied commanders would have a good sense of the French response. The harbour attack could thus be cancelled if the French strongly resisted the landings, or if they surrendered, in which case it would be unnecessary. Fritz knew that this change in timing eliminated the element of surprise, making a risky mission even more hazardous. A loudspeaker announcement as the cutters broke into the harbour would emphasize that the ships and men arriving were friends from America. The mission was at a further disadvantage if the French resisted because the strong contingent of British warships offshore was not going to bombard the harbour or shore defences in advance of the attack, partly because they did not want to antagonize the French, but also because they wanted the port facilities to be in good shape for the needs of the invasion.

Chapter Eleven

October 1942
Leaving Scotland for a 'Party' in Algeria

Always do everything you ask of those you command.

— General George S. Patton Jr.

Originally Fritz's role was to be only in planning and training, but when it became clear that the risks were enormous he assigned himself — with Admiral Cunningham's approval — to go on the lead ship *Walney*.[1] He would be on *Walney* as mission commander, but the ship's skipper was Lt.-Cdr. Cmdr. Peter Meyrick, RN. The mission had three objectives: to capture the shore batteries, to capture and hold the wharves and to board the ships in Oran harbour to prevent sabotage. The landing of troops directly from the cutters was extremely risky, but it was hoped that either the French would be taken by surprise or they would actually cooperate with the landing forces.

As Group Commander of the whole operation, Fritz was in charge of the cutters HMS *Walney* and HMS *Hartland*, motor launches 480 and 483 for laying smoke to screen the attack, the boarding parties and the landing of troops. The cutters, distinctly American in appearance and with strong ice-breaking hulls, were fitted in Belfast in mid-October with armour plating. Also, jagged blades were established on their bows for breaking through the harbour barriers.

Meanwhile, Fritz was overseeing secret training on the west coast of Scotland in preparation for the invasion, including boarding warships with grappling hooks and lines in the dark. At the Royal Navy base in Greenock, he found himself across the Firth of Clyde from Dunbartonshire where his great-grandfather, Col. Robert Gray, grew up. Shortly before embarking for the two-week voyage to the Mediterranean, he encountered his boyhood friend, Rear Admiral Frederick Dalrymple-Hamilton, who later recalled Fritz told him he couldn't say where he was going, but he was looking forward to "a party".[2]

Fritz and lady friend Dorothy Burgess on a visit to Cleish Castle in Scotland, about 1941.

In Scotland, Fritz also enjoyed meeting up with Commander David 'Solly' Joel, RN, a close friend from three decades earlier at the China Station. Joel witnessed Fritz's arrival at Greenock in a truck filled with explosives, and in command of a French gunboat similarly equipped. The two old friends spent three days together, "and the Mess ran dry," according to Joel. The extended drinking and storytelling did not seem to have any effect on Fritz, though several times Joel's secretary was sent out to buy bicarbonate of soda for him. Fritz told Joel he was personally briefed on the mission by Prime Minister Churchill, but would not say where he was going. His last words to Joel were: "Solly, I am probably going to be killed, but it's worth it."[3]

The two 1,546-ton, 256-foot-long cutters formerly used for U.S. Coast Guard patrols sailed out for the mission on October 23rd. To avoid U-boats and mask their destination, the cutters and other vessels in the invading force from Scotland sailed far to the west of Ireland before turning to the southeast. At the same time, other ships with British and American troops for the invasion were leaving various ports in Britain and Chesapeake Bay on the U.S. east coast. Amazingly, the destination of the massive armada of about 750 ships carrying 125,000 men was kept secret from the enemy, partly because the Germans were preoccupied with gigantic battles at Stalingrad, and the French and Italians assumed the Allied force was headed elsewhere in the Mediterranean. Hitler and other top Nazis were also distracted by activities associated with the anniversary of the attempted coup known as the Beer Hall Putsch in Munich on November 8, 1923.

WAR CORRESPONDENT ON BOARD

One of the Americans Fritz encountered on *Walney* was United Press International correspondent Leo Disher, who was accompanying the U.S. troops to record the first American fighting in the European Theatre. Disher wrote later that Fritz was extremely apprehensive about having a reporter on board. He carefully checked Disher's credentials and orders, and continued to be suspicious about him for several days into the voyage to Oran. Meeting new officers on board, Disher wrongly assumed a man in an American uniform was British, leading Fritz to say "Ah! If you were a spy that would have been a fatal blunder."

After leaving a planning meeting in London, Disher heard Fritz say quietly, "I hope I can see this through, but the chances of coming out alive are slim."[4] Disher noted Capt. Peters was "not new to strange missions", although it appears Disher and other Americans did not know much about Fritz's background.

For instance, the fact that he was Canadian was not mentioned in American articles, correspondence or memos. Fritz had a mid-Atlantic accent as a result of his boyhood at school in England, so his Canadian background would not have been obvious. Also, Disher said Fritz served 37 years in the Royal Navy, not realizing that he broke service twice with retirements, rejoining at the start of both world wars.

Fascinated by the enigmatic mission commander Peters, Disher wrote:

> "His courage was massive, like his shoulders. In appearance he was strikingly calm, almost annoyingly so, and the years had given him a deliberateness which made his speech as ponderous as his body. Physically, he was well-timbered, perhaps more full-bodied than portly. A deliberate man, he wore black battle dress with epaulettes

on his shoulders. He had about him a sort of stubborn pride that caused him, on land or sea, in fair weather or foul, to razor his cheeks and jowls so closely that they had a blood sheen. He was a bachelor, snugly and smugly so."[5]

Disher never figured out what made Fritz tick, but felt an aura of mystery and foreboding about him: "The mist, like rain, darkness and secrecy, followed him. And he would have one or the other, or all three, with him to the very last".[6]

DESTINATION REVEALED IN STAGES

Departing Greenock, Disher and others on board were kept in the dark as to *Walney*'s destination and mission, learning only in stages of the direction the ship was heading. Disher noted the ship listed to one side because of heavy ammunition and depth charges piled high inside her. It was bad enough to cause skipper Meyrick to suffer seasickness.

One evening Fritz came into the wardroom and sat down near Disher. "Tomorrow morning you [will] see the might of England," he said with a great sweep with his arm, "the might of England spread out on the sea." As expected, in the morning the correspondent witnessed miles of warships of many sizes in every direction. He knew *Walney* was part of a great modern Armada, but could only guess at its destination or purpose. One clue was the weather getting warmer. The personnel on board were told the mission would likely involve small arms fire, so target practice using pistols and machine guns was encouraged. There was a steady noise every day from men firing at empty tin cans thrown overboard.

Every night Fritz followed the same routine — two drinks and constantly smoking slim cheroot cigars, often lit for him by chief of staff, Lt. Paul Duncan, RN. He talked extensively on many topics — except where *Walney* was going and what lay in store for those aboard. Then, as the ship was steaming towards the British base at Gibraltar, he told officers and Disher that *Walney* and a sister ship were going to seize a harbour as part of a gigantic military operation. There were seven shore batteries and seven warships in the harbour, in addition to armed auxiliary vessels. The mission was to seize and prevent the ships from scuttling. While the ships were of value if taken over by the Allies, what was most important was to get control of the harbour in good shape so it could be used immediately for delivery of Allied supplies.

As word got around the ship of the extreme danger of the mission, poker playing intensified among the troops, with higher and higher bets and IOUs.

93

Chapter Twelve

November 6, 1942
Troublesome Rendezvous in Gibraltar

We be all good Englishmen,
Let us bang these dogs of Seville, the children of the devil,
For I never turn'd my back upon Don or devil yet.

— "The Revenge: A Ballad of the Fleet" by
Lord Alfred Tennyson

On November 5th, the Allies discreetly landed supplies of sten guns, grenades, revolvers and radio sets on the Algerian coast for use by the pro-Allied resistance during the upcoming landings. These were to support a pro-Allied coup or at least a passive reaction of defenders in Algeria to the upcoming Allied invasion, but the recipients were kept in the dark about any specific plans.

Meanwhile, *Walney* and *Hartland* were nearing the entrance to the Mediterranean at the Straits of Gibraltar. Approaching the rendezvous point of Gibraltar, the overloaded *Walney* ran aground and had to be towed free. Fritz was concerned about two engine problems on *Walney* that took time to repair earlier in the voyage.

The ship was taking on more troops at Gibraltar for the harbour attack, and could not afford any more engine failures. Fritz ordered everyone transferred to a destroyer that was standing by. Crew on *Walney* began the long and unpleasant process of transferring men, ammunition and supplies to the destroyer.

Disher described a conversation he had with the ship's chief engineer immediately after a tense meeting the chief had with Fritz in the captain's cabin soon after the transfer started. "The old boy [Captain Peters] said, 'Chief, what you're about to say is the most important thing you ever said in your life. We are headed for Oran. We are going to break the boom at Oran harbour. Do you understand? We are going in with two old Coast Guard cutters and two motor launches under the guns of seven French shore batteries and eight warships. We are going to land commando and American troops and naval ratings, capture the fort and board the warships. Hundreds of lives depend on what you say. If you say these old engines won't make it, we will transfer to a destroyer. If you say they will, we go ahead. And if they don't, so help me God, I'll have you court-martialled."[1]

The chief engineer's response was, "Sir, on my professional honour . . . they'll take us there." Fritz ordered a halt to the transfer to the destroyer, and the process was reversed back to *Walney*, a decision that brought cheers from the men tasked with the unloading and loading.

In Gibraltar, the ships picked up soldiers of the 3rd Battalion of the U.S. 6th Armored Infantry Regiment commanded by Col. George F. Marshall (not to be confused with Gen. Marshall in Washington). Unlike other Americans who opposed Operation Reservist, Marshall described it as "the finest assignment".[2]

After announcing the concept of the mission but not the location, Fritz told Disher, "Somewhere in the port, on a high hill, is a fort. I will capture that fort and send an ultimatum to the town to surrender." Fritz seemed confident saying it could be done, possibly without firing a shot. Disher said Fritz's eyes glowed as he remarked, "This is my meat. I don't feel my best until I smell the smoke of battle. Then I really begin to live!"[3]

As those listening silently calculated their chances of survival, Fritz quipped that at least the water was warm and there were no sharks. More seriously, he said intelligence wasn't sure of the condition of the boom of logs, coal barges and chains protecting the harbour they had to break through. If the cutters failed to break through, an explosives expert was standing by ready to blow the barrier apart with dynamite.

"NOBLE SIX HUNDRED"

The high risk of the mission led some on board to comment on the coincidence of the number of men for Operation Reservist — about 600, the size of a small battalion — and of the "noble six hundred" honoured in the poem *The Charge of the Light Brigade,* by Lord Alfred Tennyson about the ill-fated British cavalry charge at Balaclava in the Crimean War. Among other similarities, they were going to charge through the harbour boom with lightly-armoured cutters, as opposed to heavily-armoured destroyers. The target landing site for *Walney* was near the far west end of the 3,000-yard-wide harbour — about "half a league" in distance from the entrance boom they were smashing through. Many soldiers and sailors of the time could barely read or write, but even they were probably familiar with the famous opening line: "Half a league, half a league, half a league onward...".

Disher noted that some men on *Walney* enjoyed the black humour of reciting lines from the poem as the ship steamed towards Oran. If the French chose to resist, *Walney* and other craft in Operation Reservist would face the modern equivalent of Tennyson's famous lines about cannon fire coming from all directions.

Capt. Peters shortly before Oran mission, 1942. "A gentle smile of great charm."

CHAPTER THIRTEEN

NOVEMBER 8, 1942
AN ENTERPRISE OF DESPERATE HAZARDS

Storm'd at with shot and shell,
Boldly they rode and well,
Into the jaws of Death,
Into the mouth of Hell
Rode the six hundred.

— "The Charge of the Light Brigade" by
Lord Alfred Tennyson

Writing his news story during the evening of November 7th as *Walney* steamed towards Oran, Disher noted that the officers in the ship wardroom were amazingly calm: "This might be a fashionable club room back in New York of London . . . . The men are deep in the easy chairs, their legs hooked over the sides, reading and smoking . . . . There are no jitters aboard this ship."[1]

A report arrived saying there were now eight French warships in the harbour, including a cruiser-type destroyer tied up at the west end of the harbour where *Walney* aimed to dock. Col. Marshall announced they were going to board the largest destroyer with grappling irons.

Once given the final go ahead, the cutters were to break through the protective boom lying across the 160-yard-wide mouth of the harbour. Intelligence reports were uncertain as to the strength of the boom. If the barrier was rock solid, it might rip out *Walney*'s bottom on impact.

Once inside the long, rectangular harbour, *Hartland* was to draw fire while *Walney* proceeded west to the far end of the harbour and unloaded Special Boat Section (SBS) canoes.

These were similar in size to recreational canoes, but sturdier and with specialized equipment and motorized mines. Their use was meant to take the French warships by surprise.

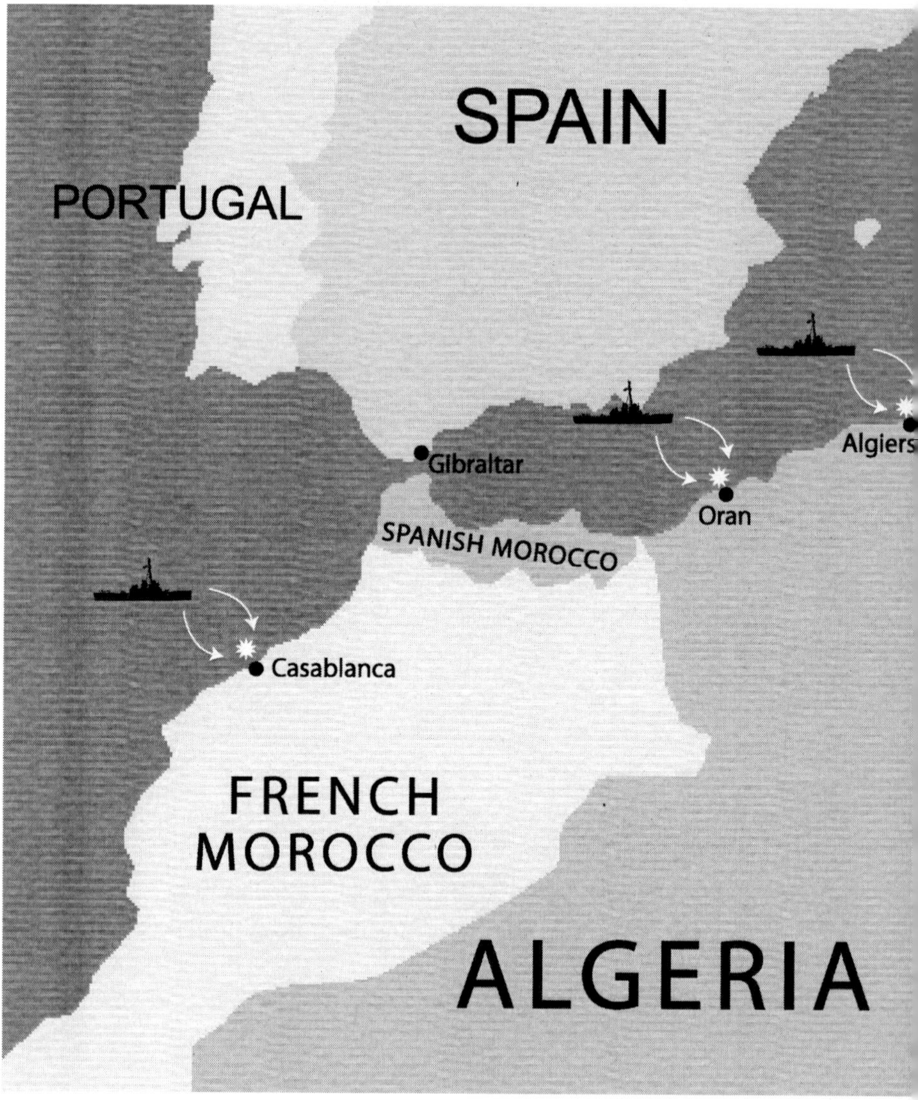
SPAIN
PORTUGAL
Gibraltar
Oran
Algiers
SPANISH MOROCCO
Casablanca
FRENCH
MOROCCO
ALGERIA

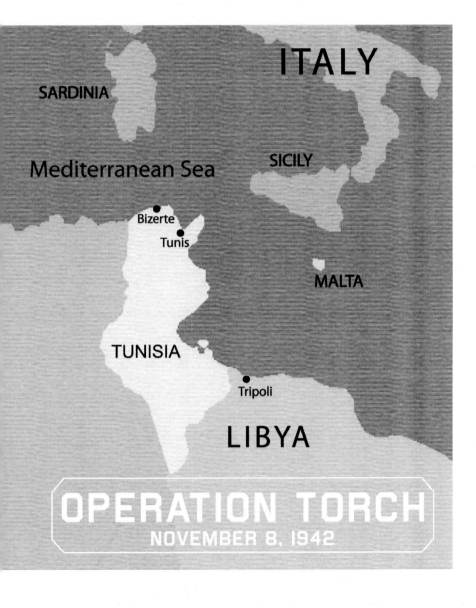

SARDINIA

ITALY

Mediterranean Sea   SICILY

●Bizerte
  ●Tunis

MALTA

TUNISIA

●Tripoli

LIBYA

OPERATION TORCH
NOVEMBER 8, 1942

IMPERSONATING AMERICANS

In light of French resentment against Britain — particularly in Oran where military personnel and residents were still furious at the British for inflicting heavy casualties at nearby Mers-el-Kebir a couple of years earlier — efforts were made to make all ships and men appear as American as possible. Churchill gave Fritz and other British commanders in Operation Torch the option of wearing American uniforms and no British markings on their ships, but he declined.

There were some things you just did not ask Fritz Peters to do, and impersonating an American was one of them. As they approached Oran, the cutters flew Stars and Stripes flags but also, defiantly, the white ensign of the Royal Navy. The British wore their regular uniforms, but it was hard to identify specific individuals because faces were blackened with grease for the attack.

The cutters approached Oran in complete darkness with no moon, accompanied by the motor launches. At first they could see the lights of Oran in the distance, but at about 2:45 a.m., the city blacked out. After the cutters were spotted by shore batteries in the hills, those on board could hear sporadic fire in the distance and see tracer bullets fired in their vicinity.

The reaction of the French continued to be crucial to the outcome of the mission. Arriving at Oran, Fritz and U.S. Col. Marshall expected to see the results of a pro-Allied coup organized to coincide with the invasion by American consul Murphy and his staff, as well as the American spy agency, the Office of Strategic Services (OSS). However, momentum for the coup stalled when a French officer originally supporting the coup got cold feet and flipped back to pro-Vichy. Unfortunately, a coded alert to "expect resistance everywhere" never got to Peters and Marshall.[2]

BEACH LANDINGS MET LITTLE RESISTANCE

In the previous couple of hours, the landings of troops on beaches to the west and east of Oran met less resistance than expected, including a barracks U.S. soldiers found to be unguarded and filled with French soldiers fast asleep. They were either incredibly incompetent or looking forward to capture. The communication from Commodore Troubridge and Gen. Fredendall on the headquarters ship HMS *Largs* was: "No shooting so far. Landings unopposed. Don't start a fight unless you have to." This confusing message drew puzzled laughter from Fritz and his colleagues on the *Walney* bridge. As it wasn't a precise order to hold off on the attack, Fritz assumed the mission was a 'go' and the final attack decision was in his hands.

Led by *Walney*, with *Hartland* and motor launches behind, the task force sailed eastward past Oran to get a good angle for colliding with the boom. The first attempt was off course, and it appeared *Walney* had turned out to sea to avoid French shelling. Disher noticed Fritz and skipper Meyrick in close discussion, then heard Meyrick announce, "Turn her . . . we're going back!"

With searchlights from shore illuminating the *Walney* deck as the ship turned in a tight circle to launch a second run to break the boom, Lt. Paul Duncan, RN, announced on a loudspeaker in American-accented French: "Don't shoot. We are your friends. We are Americans." Duncan was an astounding sight, wearing an American helmet and combat gear, two six-shooter pistols in high Western cowboy holsters and a Tommy gun under each arm, apparently to appear to the French as an American cowboy/gangster stereotype.[3] Duncan repeated his message with French fire coming his way as the cutter moved to full speed directly at the boom, until the French fire killed him as he was speaking.

INTO THE "MOUTH OF HELL"

The second run at the boom was right on target. Steaming at top speed of 15 knots, *Walney* easily smashed through the outer barrier of logs and chains and then an inner boom of coal barges. Following behind, *Hartland* crashed into the breakwater but was able to back off and make it through the opening created by *Walney*. *Hartland*'s canoes were destroyed by French bullets, but *Walney* successfully lowered its three SBS canoes with their crews and supplies in spite of fire from several anti-aircraft guns. One of the motor launches collided with *Walney* in the smoke and darkness and had to retreat outside the harbour with a damaged bow.

Walney was fortunate for a few moments after entering the harbour because the artificial smoke put out by the launches worked well in a favourable wind to hide it from the guns on shore and French warships. Also, darkness was maintained when French searchlights were shot out, and defenders turned their focus to *Hartland*.

Continuing through the harbour, Fritz saw the minesweeper sloop *La Surprise* get in *Walney*'s way when it left its moorings to investigate reports of beach landings. Fritz ordered Meyrick to ram it, but he missed because the cutter was not as manoeuvrable as the destroyers he was used to. *Surprise* didn't fire at *Walney*, but nearby destroyer *Tornade* launched a full broadside from just yards away, with two shells through *Walney*'s hull causing heavy casualties and damaging the lubricating oil tanks required for the propulsion system. As *Walney* moved slowly towards the far west end of the harbour, the 2,200-ton destroyer leader (referred to in many accounts as a cruiser) *Epervier* and a smaller destroyer *Tramontaine* opened fire. *Tramontaine* scored direct hits on *Walney*'s wardroom which killed medical staff and patients they were treating. Shells also hit the captain's cabin and the steering compartment. Another shell killed 14 of 17 men on the ship's bridge, including skipper Meyrick. The only survivors on the *Walney* bridge were Fritz Peters, correspondent Disher and a lieutenant, each severely wounded. Other shells killed most of the engine room personnel and dozens of American soldiers on the mess deck. *Walney* returned fire as best it could, knocking out *Epervier*'s searchlight and wounding several French gunners. Two French submarines moored in the harbour joined in the shelling of *Walney*.

Even with its engines destroyed, *Walney* continued to drift slowly toward its target landing site. Men on both sides of the battle were amazed to see hefty, middle-aged Fritz Peters scrambling from one end of the ship to the other, doing the work of dead or injured crew members. Despite suffering a serious head wound, he made his way from the bridge to tie a mooring line to an adjacent jetty. Shooting from machine guns and pistols and lobbing grenades, Fritz and other survivors continued to exchange fire with Frenchmen on *Epervier* for almost an hour before flames on *Walney* forced them away from their guns.[4]

MIRACULOUS ARRIVAL AT DESTINATION

Amazingly, *Walney* arrived close to its target berth and succeeded in landing some men, but they were immediately captured and taken prisoner. Ammunition and depth charges on *Walney* began exploding. With flames everywhere, orders went out to abandon ship. The sister ship *Hartland* suffered a similar fate. Both mangled ships were torn apart by explosions and eventually sank in the harbour. Some French defenders were helpful in rescuing survivors, but others machine-gunned them as they struggled helpless in the water.

Fritz swam to an inflated raft and made it to shore with other men in the raft. There he encountered a French soldier with a machine gun and "took care of him with his pistol", according to his friend Swain Saxton in a 1943 interview with the *London Evening Standard*. As Fritz was taken prisoner, he announced he was in command and demanded to see the officer in charge, Admiral André Rioult. Their meeting immediately developed into a shouting match about who fired first, with Fritz letting him have it in his "fractured French".

As he sat waiting to be marched to prison, Fritz wore a black eyepatch over his injured eye and was described as a hatless and dejected buccaneer. He led other survivors in a march first to a civil prison and later to a military prison through the streets of Oran, with residents along the way jeering and spitting at them.

Many American witnesses who later recommended Fritz for the U.S. Distinguished Service Cross applauded him for remaining on the bridge in command even though the protective armour had been blown in by enemy shellfire, exposing him to crossfire. "He accomplished the berthing of his ship, then went to the forward deck and, assisted by one officer, secured the forward mooring lines. He then, with utter disregard for his own safety, went to the quarterdeck and assisted in securing the aft mooring lines so the troops on board could disembark," according to the citation for the U.S. DSC.

COURAGE AND LEADERSHIP PRAISED

In recommending Fritz for the Victoria Cross, Adm. Cunningham said: "The vital element of surprise having failed, it developed into an enterprise of desperate hazard, but although blinded in one eye he led his force to their objective through point blank fire from shore batteries and ships in harbour. His courage and leadership achieved all that could be done against odds that proved overwhelming."

After destroying the two cutters, the French warships headed out of the harbour to attack the troop ships, but once out to sea the odds were reversed, and the British warships offshore were no longer restrained. The full fury of the Royal Navy was unleashed on the French ships, sinking *La Surprise* and causing *Tramontaine*, *Tornade* and later *Epervier* to run aground. Severely damaged, *Typhon* was able to make it back to Oran harbour where it was scuttled to block the entrance.

TWICE THE CASUALTY RATE OF THE CHARGE OF THE LIGHT BRIGADE

The casualty numbers were staggering. Of 393 U.S. soldiers on board the two cutters, 183 died and 157 were wounded. There were 113 Royal Navy dead and 86 wounded as well as five U.S. navy dead and seven wounded. The casualty rate was 90 per cent — about double the casualty rate of the Charge of the Light Brigade in the Crimea 88 years earlier.[5]

When Oran surrendered to advancing American troops two days after the landings, the port was littered with the wrecks of more than 20 ships, including *Walney* and *Hartland*. To spite the invaders, the French had scuttled most of their ships so as to block access within the harbour. They were about to spread oil in the harbour and set it on fire when American soldiers stopped them.

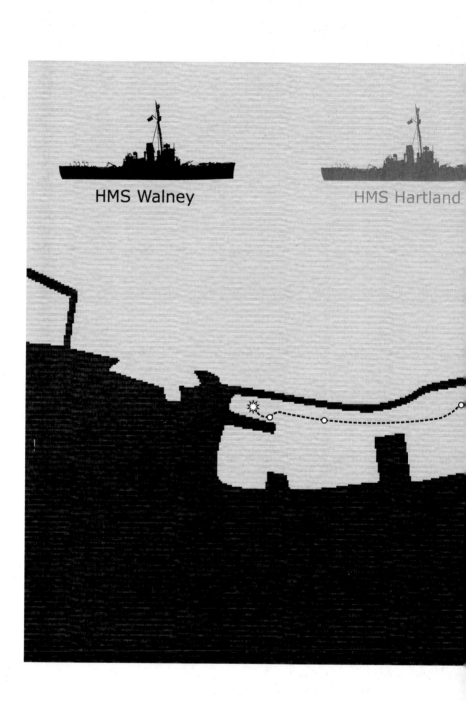

HMS Walney

HMS Hartland

Walney

Hartland

ATTACK OF
HMS WALNEY & HMS HARTLAND
IN ORAN HARBOUR

A similar attack on Algiers harbour also failed, but with 'only' 23 killed and 51 wounded, and the harbour was left in better shape than Oran harbour. In Morocco, the Safi harbour south of Casablanca was successfully captured by two destroyers, at a cost of four dead and 25 wounded. Americans who celebrated the Safi victory pointed out it was significantly different from the disastrous British-led attacks at Oran and Algiers because the Safi harbour attack slightly preceded the nearby beach landings so as to benefit from surprise, Safi's shore defences were weaker, there were no French warships present and the American destroyers had fire support from other ships.

An audacious attempt by a battalion of American parachute infantry flying all the way from England badly missed its Oran target landing site after encountering storms over Spain.

While the high-risk, spectacular missions failed, the overall invasion went well and had fewer casualties than expected. The strategy of landing troops outside of Oran and Algiers and then attacking them from each flank and behind worked well. However, as the first combined operation of Britain and America, the invasion exposed numerous shortcomings of the Allied forces. For instance, many of the shells from American warships failed to explode — a result of sitting in storage since the First World War. Both Gen. Eisenhower and Gen. Patton later said they would have been in serious trouble if they had been up against Germans in Operation Torch rather than half-hearted Frenchmen.

Soon after the city surrendered at noon on Tuesday, November 10th, U.S. soldiers arrived at the prison and set Fritz and other survivors free. Many Oran residents quickly changed their allegiance to support the Allies. Fritz was carried on shoulders in triumph in an impromptu parade through the streets of Oran. In addition to flowers thrown towards the parading victors, one enthusiastic onlooker threw an orange to Fritz as a tribute. It hit him in the face, resulting in a black eye to go along with the eyepatch protecting his other eye, which had been injured in the harbour attack. He would soon leave for England via the base at Gibraltar to report on the mission and receive medical treatment.

CHAPTER FOURTEEN
FRIDAY THE 13TH

. . .Not tho' the soldier knew
Someone had blunder'd. . .
. . .Then they rode back, but not,
Not the six hundred.

— "The Charge of the Light Brigade" by
Lord Alfred Tennyson

It was Friday, November 13, 1942, and the negative connotations of the date were not lost on Fritz Peters. Climbing on the Sunderland flying boat in Gibraltar at 7:30 a.m. for a day-long flight back to England, he joked to the Royal Australian Air Force (RAAF) crew: "You know, us Navy men are superstitious. We really shouldn't be flying on Friday the 13th!" [1]

At Eisenhower's headquarters in Gibraltar, Fritz may have heard of the sinking the day before of the anti-aircraft ship HMS *Tynwald*, which he had commanded for a year before transferring to Operation Torch in August 1942.

Tynwald went down on November 12, 1942, with 10 sailors dead near Bougie in eastern Algeria, sunk by either a mine or torpedo from an Italian submarine. This was perhaps another bad omen for Fritz, whose long string of good luck — which had enabled him to survive hundreds of close calls in his life — was about to end.

The RAAF crew were looking forward to an easier trip than the flight out to Gibraltar from Plymouth three days earlier, when their overloaded flying boat barely made it into the air at takeoff, and passengers were ordered not to move at all for the first part of the flight. The supply of fuel was supposed to be reduced to allow for a heavier than normal load for the flight, but a crew member mistakenly filled it with fuel, an error that almost resulted in a court martial.[2]

CHURCHILL AWAITED HIS REPORT

Fritz was being rushed back to England to brief Winston Churchill on what happened in Oran harbour. More amphibious invasions lay ahead for the Allies in their strategy for defeating Hitler, and a key factor in the success of the landings would be access to usable harbours as quickly as

RAAF pilot Wynton Thorpe, about 1942, who valiantly attempted to carry Fritz to safety in the frigid sea for more than an hour. Photo courtesy of Col. Brooke Thorpe.

possible. Churchill wanted to hear from Fritz what worked and what didn't, and what changes they should make for the next landings.

The crew of the Sunderland flying boat was from the No. 10 Squadron of the RAAF who flew out of the Mount Batten base near Plymouth mainly for anti-sub patrols but also for transporting VIPs. The primary purpose of the flight was to transport five VIPs back to England, but the crew also intended to do reconnaissance in the Bay of Biscay along the way.

PERFECT STORM OF BAD CONDITIONS

As it turned out, disaster awaited the Sunderland due to a combination of bad luck, bad weather forecasting and a faulty altimeter. Calm conditions were predicted as the flight left Gibraltar, but it turned out to be almost a perfect storm of hostile weather. Shortly after takeoff, they ran into 40-knot headwinds and later lightning, hail and sleet. It made for an exceptionally bumpy ride for passengers, particularly Fritz, who had only received rudimentary treatment for the array of injuries he'd suffered five days before in Oran harbour, including a damaged eye, injured shoulder and numerous shrapnel wounds to his body. Much of the craft's fuel was used up flying through the stormy weather early in the flight.

"After we'd reached the point of no return we ran into the thickest fog I'd ever seen and the night was as black as the inside of a cat," the pilot, Flight Officer Wynton Thorpe, said in a 1987 interview.[3]

Seven and a half hours into the flight, Thorpe radioed saying the flying boat might be forced to land outside the Plymouth breakwater. At 7:50 p.m., more than 12 hours into the flight, he sent another message saying the Sunderland had less than 15 minutes of fuel. Thorpe approached the flare path going into Mount Batten base but overshot in heavy fog and circled to make a second attempt. His second approach was completely blinded by fog so he relied on the plane's altimeter. At 7:56, he saw the altimeter read an altitude of 600 feet, just as the Sunderland slammed into the sea.

Because the starboard wing was lower at the time of impact, the flying boat flipped over and split apart about a mile and a half from the breakwater. None of the five passengers would survive the crash but, miraculously, all 11 of the crew survived, though three suffered serious injuries. "The first thing I remembered after impact was being in the icy sea," recalled Thorpe, who was shaken up from the landing but unhurt. Close to him in the water was Capt. Peters, who Thorpe found to be unconscious but the only passenger still alive.[4] Thorpe, 23, grabbed on to Fritz and towed him along while swimming to the breakwater. Completely exhausted after about an hour, Thorpe saw Fritz was definitely dead and let go of the body. The survivors were picked up by a rescue boat about half an hour later.

The same rough weather around Gibraltar that caused Fritz's flight to get off to a terrible start also threatened Eisenhower and his deputy commander Cunningham when they flew that same day from Algiers to Allied headquarters in Gibraltar. Eisenhower wrote later: "I saw no way out of a bad predicament and still think the young lieutenant pilot must have depended more upon a rabbit's foot than upon his controls to accomplish the skilful landing that finally brought us safely down."[5] The experience led Eisenhower to speed up plans to shift headquarters from Gibraltar to Algiers, even though communications facilities were not ready.

Eisenhower would go on to be Supreme Commander of the Western Allies for the rest of the war, and serve as President of the United States between 1953 and 1961.

BAD NEWS VIA TELEGRAMS

Two days after the crash, on Sunday, November 15, 1942, Helen Dewdney at home in Nelson was startled to hear a CBC radio news report that "Captain T.F. Peters" of the Royal Navy had died in a plane crash along with Brigadier Vogel. The initials of his name were transposed, but otherwise it sounded like her brother Fritz. She had no idea where Fritz was stationed, but thought it was likely he was in command of a ship. Helen contacted the local newspaper and asked if they could get more details on the crash. The *Nelson Daily News* passed on the inquiry to the Associated Press, who in turn contacted the British Admiralty. Two days later, Bertha Peters received a telegram from the Admiralty saying they "deeply regret to confirm that your son Acting Captain Frederic Thornton Peters DSO, DSC reported as missing presumed killed on 13 November when aircraft in which he was travelling from North Africa crashed at Plymouth South Devon." A second telegram received later in the afternoon added further condolences.[6]

News that two small Allied warships sank in Oran harbour was covered in the November 9, 1942, newspapers in Canada and the U.S., but further details were slow to arrive. A week after the attack, the *New York Times* reported "rugged seafarer" Capt. Peters was the only survivor of one of the sunken vessels. A day later, the *Times* reported an announcement from Gen. Eisenhower that Capt. Peters had died in a plane crash and was recommended for the Distinguished Service Cross for gallantry in the attack on Oran harbour. Another victim of the crash was Brig. Frank Vogel, a British officer serving on Eisenhower's staff.

CHAPTER FIFTEEN

AFTERMATH
SILENCE IS THE BEST POLICY

I have fought for Queen and Faith like a valiant man and true;
I have only done my duty as a man is bound to do.
With a joyful spirit I, Sir Richard Grenville, die!

— "The Revenge: A Ballad of the Fleet" by
Lord Alfred Tennyson

In retrospect, the lacklustre reaction of defenders on the beaches around
Oran was not a valid predictor of the response in the city's harbour, where
defenders had the advantages of an established fort, and there were political
and military leaders loyal to Vichy on hand to counteract any attempts at
a coup, or to surrender. One of the consequences of the extremely tight
secrecy of the invasion was that pro-Allied groups in Algeria who may have
been able to help the Allies in the attack were kept in the dark about it,
along with everyone else.

Adm. Cunningham later acknowledged "the moment chosen [for the
harbour attack] could hardly have been less fortunate, since the French
alarm to arms was in its first flush of Gallic fervour and they had not
yet been intimidated by bombing or bombardment, whilst darkness
prevented any American complexion to the operation being apparent."[1]
Gen. Eisenhower accepted responsibility for the mistake in timing of
Operation Reservist at the Casablanca Conference, attended by Roosevelt
and Churchill in January 1943.

"We discovered the actual state of French sentiment in North Africa did
not even remotely agree with some of our prior calculations," Eisenhower
said in an After Action Report in May 1943. He noted that by the time
French forces joined up with the Allies on November 18, 1942, "it was too
late to overcome the fatal effects of the almost morbid sense of honour
which had led the French initially to resist us, their deliverers, while they
were leaving their back door open to the enemy." [2] The back door was the
French colony of Tunisia, immediately south of Axis-held Sicily.

ALLIED FORCE HEADQUARTERS
Office of the Commander-in-Chief

29 November 1942

Secretary of the Admiralty,
London, England.

Dear Sir:

There is inclosed two copies of my general order awarding the Distinguished Service Cross to the late Captain F. T. Peters, DSO, DSC, retired, Royal Navy, for extraordinary heroism during the attack on Oran, Morocco, in the early morning of 8 November 1942. The medal itself is being sent under separate cover.

The recommendation for this decoration was initiated by Major General Fredendall, who commanded the Center Task Force during the operation, and was in process in my headquarters at the time I learned of the tragic accident which resulted in the death of Captain Peters, therefore, the award is not indicated as posthumous.

Please convey to Captain Peters' family my deepest sympathy in the loss of their kinsman and gallant officer, and my regret that I am unable to present the decoration to them personally.

Faithfully yours,

DWIGHT D. EISENHOWER
Lieutenant General, U. S. A.,
Commander-in-Chief

On November 9th, Germans began landing men and supplies in Tunisia to stop the Allies from securing all of North Africa. French defenders were supposed to fend off all invaders, including Germans, but, in sharp contrast to what happened at Oran harbour, they took no action to stop the Germans. Jean-Pierre Esteva, French resident-general, Tunisia, and Vice Adm. Edmond-Louis Derrien, French military commander at the key Tunisian port of Bizerte, were later prosecuted in French courts for their inaction against the Germans and sentenced to life imprisonment. Derrien later said he would also not have resisted the arrival of Allied troops at Bizerte.

There were never any apologies from the French about their actions at Oran harbour, including the shooting of survivors in the water. One Oran official had the gall to send the Allies a bill for *Walney's* and *Hartland's* pilotage fees, as if they were regular commercial users of the harbour.[3]

To their credit, the French lived up to their promise of not allowing the Germans to take over warships in France's main naval base of Toulon on the Mediterranean coast. On November 27, 1942, with Germans rushing to take over the ships, French sailors skilfully scuttled the entire fleet to avoid transfer of ships to the German or Italian navies.

INVASION SUPPLY NEEDS LEAD TO ARTIFICIAL MULBERRY HARBOURS

At liberated Oran, the British and French were impressed to see the fast work of can-do American engineers in rehabilitating the harbour to be in full working order by the first week of January 1943. By then, however, the Germans had won the race to Tunisia, where they put up a determined defence until finally defeated by the Allies in May 1943. In addition to delaying the Allies' progress in the European Theatre, the battles in Tunisia resulted in 70,000 Allied casualties.

While U.S. Adm. Bennett did well in charge of harbour restoration at Oran, he antagonized Eisenhower by continuing to harp about British mistakes in Operation Reservist. He eventually was transferred to distant Iceland.[4]

Like the disastrous Dieppe Raid of August 1942, the easy sabotaging of Oran harbour by defenders was a lesson to the Allies that they could not count on using existing port facilities in subsequent amphibious invasions. The pressing need for delivery of reinforcements and supplies led to the innovation of Mulberry artificial harbours for the Normandy Invasion of June 1944. These involved pre-fabricated structures towed to target beaches and sunk into place with thousands of tons of concrete to establish temporary harbours with calm water for landing supplies. One of the two Mulberries was destroyed by a storm just 10 days after installation, but the other lasted for 10 months and enabled the delivery of huge amounts of supplies.

Harbours continued to be crucial to the success of Allied advances for the rest of the war. By clearing German forces from the Scheldt Estuary in November 1944, Canadian troops had a key role in enabling the great natural port of Antwerp to be used for the massive Allied assault on Germany.

GEN. FREDENDALL EXPOSED

On November 18, 1942, U.S. Gen. Fredendall, commander of the Centre Task Force, pinned a Purple Heart medal on war correspondent Leo Disher, who sustained serious injuries in the Oran action but miraculously survived. Disher's survival was even more remarkable because he was hobbling along on crutches and had a leg in a cast as a result of breaking an ankle from a fall on the *Walney* deck before arriving in the Mediterranean.

Aside from the heavy casualties in the harbours of Oran and Algiers, overall casualties in the Allied conquest of Algeria were remarkably light. Fortunately, Adm. Darlan, chief of French armed forces, happened to be in Algiers on a private visit when the invaders arrived. Through him, the Allies gained an early surrender of Algiers. Most of the fighting was in Morocco, where U.S. forces led by Gen. Patton encountered fierce pockets of resistance. Patton famously put his life at risk by coming ashore early and directing traffic to overcome bottlenecks on the beaches. In contrast, Gen. Fredendall stayed safe on the headquarters ship HMS *Largs* well offshore until the fighting around Oran was all but over.

Visiting Fredendall's headquarters in eastern Algeria in February 1943, Eisenhower was astounded to see the general had used his 200 engineers to build a huge fortified underground bunker with quarters for himself safe from any possible German attack, even though the war was progressing to the east, and the engineers should have been supporting troops at the front. Fredendall had a phobia about being killed by bullets shot from planes overhead.[5] When German Gen. Rommel counterattacked Fredendall's force at Kasserine Pass a couple of weeks later, the result was one of the most humiliating defeats in American history, with U.S. troops fleeing in panic from their positions.

After the rout at Kasserine, Fredendall was replaced as commander of II Corps by Gen. Patton, a transition made famous by the 1970 movie *Patton*. The fates were kinder to Fredendall than they were to Fritz Peters. Not wanting to hurt his feelings, Eisenhower gave Fredendall a promotion and assigned him to a command in charge of training back in the States, where he was cheered in victory parades. He died in 1963 before books came out about his follies in North Africa. American historian Stephen

Ambrose said a major benefit of the North Africa invasion was the weeding out of incompetent American commanders. "The idea of Fredendall in charge [of American soldiers in desperate battle] at Omaha Beach is by itself enough to justify the Mediterranean campaign," he wrote.[6]

SILENCE IS THE BEST POLICY

On the home front, the North Africa invasion was on front pages for a while, but soon became old news as dramatic events in the war unfolded, and Allied authorities chose to downplay the invasion in public announcements.

In a memo to the Admiralty about the Oran harbour attack, dated December 18, 1942, Adm. Cunningham said, "the conduct of all who took part in this enterprise, although it failed in its purpose, conformed with the highest standards of gallantry to which the British Navy aspires in action."

Then Cunningham gave reasons for keeping quiet about the Oran incident in the interest of Allied harmony. "I have not thought it expedient to issue a communiqué on the operation," Cunningham noted, adding, "the attitude of the French both official and public may [now] be said to be almost cordial. A case has been brought to me of a French naval officer whose wife was killed by our bombardment, but who is giving courteous and valuable assistance to our naval forces at Oran. There are no doubt many similar cases, [so] for the time being I think silence is the best policy".[7]

Cunningham was apparently unaware that the weekly BBC radio report of Lt.-Cdr. (Ret.) Thomas Woodrooffe, RN, on December 3, 1942, had extensive information about the Oran harbour attack. On the night of the invasion, Woodrooffe was on a supply ship in the Gulf of Arzew about 20 miles east of Oran. From there he could see and hear signs of heavy action in the harbour, which he visited after the city surrendered. Woodrooffe saw the extensive wreckage and interviewed survivors and officials. As a retired naval officer, he was given more leeway than a regular journalist in reporting war action. In line with the secrecy requirements of the time, he did not mention Capt. Peters' name in his broadcast, but other reporters soon connected Fritz with the heroic exploits in the harbour, which foiled any plans Cunningham may have had to hush up the story[8].

ORAN HONOURS

For the Admiralty committee evaluating honours, there was no question about the Victoria Cross for Fritz Peters. The issue was whether to also award one to *Hartland* skipper Lt.-Cdr. Godfrey Billot, RNR, who managed to survive the action with minor injuries. In the thick of the harbour conflict, Billot went below to personally disable the ship's depth charges to prevent them from exploding and causing further casualties. The committee decided that the case for Fritz's VC was significantly stronger than Billot's, so Billot was honoured with the Distinguished Service Order, which also went to two surviving lieutenants. As well, there were six Distinguished Service Crosses, three Distinguished Service Medals, one Conspicuous Gallantry Medal, four Mentions in Dispatches and one posthumous Mention in Dispatch for Lt.-Cdr. Peter Meyrick[9].

Among Americans, six U.S. Distinguished Service Cross medals were awarded, five posthumously, including one for Col. Marshall who was last seen on the *Walney* deck throwing grenades at Frenchmen on *Epervier*. The United States tended to award considerably fewer honours for a failed operation than for a victory, whereas the British philosophy was that a failed enterprise could be redeemed by the gallantry of participants.[10]

In February 1943, British authorities developed a tentative statement for public release saying that Peters' VC was "for valour in taking HMS *Walney*, in an enterprise of desperate hazard, into the harbour of Oran. Capt. Peters led his force through the boom towards the jetty in the face of point blank fire from shore batteries, a destroyer and a cruiser. Blinded in one eye, he alone of seventeen officers and men on the bridge survived. The *Walney* reached the jetty, disabled and ablaze, and went down with the White Ensign and Stars and Stripes flying."

Fritz's VC was officially approved and announced in the Gazette on May 18, 1943. Concerned that the VC was getting scarce publicity because authorities were not giving out details of the Oran action, Fritz's close friend Swain Saxton visited an acquaintance who was a columnist at the *London Evening Standard* newspaper. In addition to providing more details on Oran, Saxton talked about Fritz's years at the Gold Coast colony where he foiled three attempts on his life and defended the honour of the Royal Navy against detractors.

SEARCHING FOR INFORMATION

After Fritz's death, his mother Bertha wrote numerous letters trying to learn more about the Oran action as well as Fritz's life since she last saw him in Canada in August 1919. She received the following responses from two Admirals and a British war correspondent.

The first letter was from Sir Arthur Malcolm Peters, KCB, DSC, who at the time was moving on from an appointment as Naval Secretary to the First Lord of the Admiralty. Peters — no relation to Fritz — went to sea in 1904 and rose to Admiral at his retirement in 1945. He was in the Battle of Dogger Bank in 1915, and received the Distinguished Service Cross for bravery in the Battle of Jutland in 1916. In 1943 he moved to service in the Mediterranean Fleet and then to Flag Officer, West Africa.

ADMIRAL A.M. PETERS TO BERTHA   FEBRUARY 14, 1943

Office of the Rear Admiral
Dear Mrs. Peters,

I am so glad you wrote to me about your son, as, though I cannot claim to have been a friend of his (we have only met, I think, three times, the last being some 12 years ago in Kumazi^i), he was a man whom it was a great privilege to know and whom I have always heard spoken of with admiration and affection by those who knew him better. I am afraid I can tell you little concerning his end, beyond the fact that the aircraft in which he was returning from Africa (wounded and sent home specially to make his report) crashed at sea and there were no survivors^{ii}. I can tell you a little more of his glorious deeds at Oran; he was in command of a vessel whose duty it was to break through the defences at the entrance to the harbour, and get alongside and attack certain French ships should opposition be met. There was intense opposition, his bridge was raked with machine gun fire at close range; practically everyone on the bridge except himself was killed and he was wounded. Nevertheless he held on and achieved his object, and was subsequently taken prisoner. He was taken before the French admiral, with whom (typical of him!) he entered into a fierce argument about who fired first, and upbraided the French admiral for firing on him at all. He was then kept in prison for two or three days until, after the change of attitude of the French, he was carried through the streets with acclamation, and returned to the American authorities.

His gallantry was typical of little I have seen… and is looked upon with pride and admiration by all in the navy who have heard of it. Most men of his age who have been out of the navy for some years have had to rest content with easier appointments on shore. At the beginning of the war he managed to find his way through to a sea command, and has done so again now, thus enhancing the great reputation he made for himself in the last war. You have indeed been hardly tried in losing three sons in the two wars, and, in venturing to offer my very deep sympathy, may I hope that the loss will be softened by pride in this man's glorious achievements.

His subsequent loss, after all he had been through, and done, was a terrible misfortune; it is men of his type who are winning the war for us…

A.M. Peters

i. Kumasi in Ghana of today was formerly known as Kumazi, Gold Coast Colony.
ii. He is mistaken. Survivors were discussed in Chapter 14.

Rear Adm. Frederick Dalrymple-Hamilton replaced Adm. A.M. Peters as Naval Secretary to the First Lord of the Admiralty in late 1942. He was commander of the battleship HMS *Rodney* en route to America for refitting when it was called on to join the battle against *Bismarck* in May 1941. *Rodney* exchanged shell hits with the *Bismarck* and joined other ships in sinking the German battleship. Dalrymple-Hamilton was a close lifelong friend of the Bowes-Lyon family, particularly the Queen Mother. He crossed paths with Fritz Peters many times over four decades.

REAR ADMIRAL DALRYMPLE-HAMILTON TO BERTHA   FEBRUARY 22, 1943

Admiralty Whitehall

Dear Mrs. Peters,

I enclose a letter to you from my predecessor in office Admiral A.M. Peters. I should like to endorse all he says about your son. It may interest you to know that I was at the same private school Cordwalles Maidenhead as he was. We were in the cricket eleven together, passed into the Britannia together and went to sea at the same time. I remember him back as a midshipman and later we were at Portsmouth together as sub lieutenants. In the last war I relieved him as First Lieutenant of the destroyer Meteor in the Harwich force. I had never lost touch with him and used to see him periodically on his return for leave from West Africa. The last time I saw him was by great fortune the day before he set out on the expedition to Africa [Algeria]. I had not seen him for 5 years previously but found him just the same as ever and delighted to be going to take a hand in the party. I did not know at the time what the part he had to play was to be — but from talking to him one might have thought he was going to a nice party instead of on a desperate venture.

Danger never had any bearing for him and engaging the enemy was the one thing he lived for. The President of the United States has conferred a Distinguished Service Cross on him which is a very high honour and well-deserved. I hope he may receive something from his own countrymen as well.[i] We are all proud of him.

He was in a ship called Hartland[ii] which with another was detailed to force a way into the harbour of Oran. The two ships were under his command. Although they were met with heavy fire they struggled on and reached the far end of the harbour before being sunk. Most of the men on the bridge of his ship were killed but he survived and eventually got ashore as Admiral Peters has told you. It was a very gallant effort. I believe Mrs. Varley, the wife of a great mutual friend of ours has been sent his decorations, but this I am not sure about. I will however make some inquiries. Commander Varley was in our term in the Britannia, and I think they had always been great friends. I met him and Mrs. Varley a month ago and we talked a great deal of Fritz...

Yours sincerely, F. D. Hamilton, Rear Admiral

P.S. – March 1, 1943. I have now heard from Commander Varley. He has the decorations and says he has written to you to say he would like to send them over after the war when transport is safe. This sounds a good idea but rather depends on how long the war lasts! Perhaps you could write to Commander C.H. Varley, DSO, RN at Chilworth Hill, Guildford, Surrey and say what you would like done. If there is anything more I can do please be sure and let me know.

i.   This was before Fritz was awarded the Victoria Cross.
ii. He is mistaken, as Fritz was on *Walney*, not *Hartland*.

British author and correspondent A. David Divine, author of *Road to Tunis* and *Firedrake: The Destroyer That Wouldn't Give Up*, won a Distinguished Service Cross for bravery at Dunkirk in 1940. He accompanied American troops in the Tunisian Campaign and provided eyewitness accounts of battles.

A.D. DIVINE TO BERTHA   JULY 17, 1944

24, Keats Grove, London, N.W.3

I have just received your letter on my return from Normandy ...I think I can assure you at once that Captain Peters was looked after with the utmost care from the moment of his release [from the French prison at Oran]. I know personally that the senior medical officers of General Fredendall's staff themselves attended to him at once, and that he was very comfortably housed at headquarters and given every possible attention and honour, for the Americans, like ourselves, realized that his was one of the finest deeds of the war — a piece of heroic self-sacrificing and daring.

*I saw little of him myself apart from the brief episode at the confer-
ence at the Chateau Neuf [i], but I did meet him twice afterwards at the
Grand Hotel, and I know that before he left for Gibraltar he was very
much better and his face had lost much of the look of strain and shock
that marked it when he was first released.*

*...There is so little that I can tell you, I fear, that would be of any
comfort, but I do know that the men who were with him, the survivors
of the exploit, spoke of your son in the very highest possible terms. They
would, I know, have gone with him again knowing that the same future
was in store for them. From Officers who were with him on the voyage
out too (I was in another ship) I heard story after story of his determination, his courage, and his unquenchable gaiety.*

*With regard to the tragedy of the accident at Gibraltar [ii] I know noth-
ing at all. I was by this time on the Tunisian front, and I heard the news
with a great sense of shock for I knew — as I think few others did at the
time, the brilliance and the dash of this Zeebrugge in miniature.*

*...You have for comfort the knowledge that your son was one of the
bravest men that this war has produced, and that he did for his country a
magnificent and brilliant deed.*

— A.D. Divine

i.   A historic Spanish fortress in Oran which became a military
     headquarters for the French and later the Allies.
ii. A common mistake in accounts of Fritz's life is that he died in
     an air crash near Gibraltar, but in fact the flying boat crashed
     in Plymouth Sound close to its destination.

Divine wasn't alone in describing the Oran harbour attack as a
"Zeebrugge in miniature". The famous Royal Navy raid on Zeebrugge,
Belgium, in April 1918 was designed to block the entrance to the German-
held port of Bruges with large sunken ships so U-boats and other light
ships in the port would be unable to get out to sea. It shut down the port
for a few days but Germans were eventually able to create a channel to get
subs through in high tide. Still, it was celebrated as a great British victory,
with eight Victoria Crosses awarded. Zeebrugge and Oran were actually
very different operations, as one was designed to shut down a harbour and
the other to keep the harbour open for shipping.

Bertha also received letters from retired navy officers who were among
Fritz's best friends going back to his time as a cadet or serving on the
China Station.

Paymaster-Commander Sydney W. 'Swain' Saxton, RN retired at the
end of the First World War, became a lawyer, and held a senior position

in the colonial administration as District Commissioner of the Gold Coast colony in central west Africa. As a close friend of Fritz going back to cadet days, he may have encouraged Fritz to come to Gold Coast for work after Fritz retired from the Navy in 1920. The son Saxton mentions who was a godson of Fritz was John Clifford Waring Saxton, born in 1930. In 1945 Saxton sent Bertha a signed framed photograph of Fritz that had been a gift to the godson from the godfather.

NAVAL COLLEAGUE SAXTON TO BERTHA   JUNE 6, 1943

Caynham Vicarage, Ludlow

My dear Mrs. Peters,

...If this letter remained unwritten I should be false to the ideals of friendship and false to the glorious memory of one I regarded in the light of a brother. But the object of this letter is not only to satisfy myself as to something he would have wished me to do but also to endeavour to convey to you, in some small measure, some idea of how his friends mourned his untimely death, and how deeply and sincerely we sympathize with you, his mother, so far distant from the glamour of his courageous exploits and from the spot where he viewed the last of this island he loved and served so well. Your sorrow we would share and also a little of the pride which must be yours in having borne such a son as Frederick Thornton.

The word "we" I have used purposely for it represents a community who looked upon your son as a legendary figure...

His death came as a great blow and perhaps I can epitomize the sense of void by saying "a little girl cried". It is true that she is now no longer a child but it was the child in her who wept when she found missing from the mirror of her life, a dear, always smiling and lovable "big" friend.

This was no hero worship but a tribute of simplicity to a gentle nature which survived some rather cruel buffetings in a varied life. As I have said, to we older people he was a legendary figure but here again it was no hero worship although his long list of decorations for valour would have justified a blind admiration did he not possess those higher qualities one and all would like to be judged by.

Speaking to you as his mother, I need say nothing of the nobility of his character nor of the lofty purpose of his actions at all times and under all circumstances. Where duty lay, as he conceived it, so was his set purpose and no sacrifice was too great to carry out that duty to his end.

In war this may be an easier objective than in the ordinary battle of existence. It was perseverance, energy and patience that always kept his head above adversity. The laurels of success might have come to him easily through his ability to master any difficult problem or situation and provided he was prepared to deviate from some point which to him was a matter of principle. I tried hard to try and convince him to take up the law. I had done so myself, and my risk in backing him was small for he must have soon made a name. He possessed all those qualities and personality which would have quickly taken him out of the first rut. I had met his father, and it seemed to me he had an easy ball at his feet. He would not consider this proposition because he was staggeringly in debt and he might not be able to repay me.

To those who knew him it was obvious his V.C. was struck in 1914–1918. That it came too late would constitute just a run of bad luck. As a courageous man he won his medals with humility and he regarded them as confined to and belonging to the Navy to which he was so proud to belong. It so happened we were cast together when all servicemen were regarded almost as pariahs. I argued at length with Frederick Thornton and stated he was performing a disservice to his comrades in arms in HM Navy by concealing his real identity. Although distasteful to him he permitted that recognition to which he was entitled. His was a courage born of directness of purpose, a very high ideal of tradition and HM Navy — cool and determined, he was not reckless for recklessness could never have carried him through his many dangerous moments up to Oran. His courage was of the caliber which realized danger even if fear was unknown to him.

I did not see him before Oran. A message went wrong and he searched for me the day I left London. Colonel Lawson, the third member of his trinity, was more fortunate, and was with him until he sailed. I feel badly cheated. Colonel Lawson will be writing to you. I introduced him to FTP about 1908, since then we have moved about together. Lawson and I married some 25 years ago, and your late son was a member of both our families. He had always promised to be godfather to my son when we had one; so 12 years ago he became a "family man" by proxy. Last December year I collected the boy from Toronto, brought him back to England when I retired from the Gold Coast Political Service...

It is difficult to write of a man one has known so long and whom one regarded as being a brother but I hope when we have established contact I may fill in possibly some gaps in his adventurous life. It was a fulsome one and I have not yet met anyone who did not love him or admire him. In some of his friends he was able to inspire the most blind devotion and although out of touch with the Navy this war through no fault of my own it is obvious that his was a full measure of service and devotion. My daughter who is returning from the Gold Coast to have a baby confirms that the memory of him is still more than alive in that odd corner of

Africa. ...Unfortunately through bombs I have lost many relics of F.T.P. but I think I still have some snaps...

May I finish this very inadequate letter on this great and lovable man. Frederick Thornton will have thought of Oran as his greatest adventure, in spite of his experience of other dangerous places in both wars. He will have found true the ideal of his highest tradition. To him Narvik was hell but if Oran was a war inferno he will not have thought so. The serious business will have found him cool, grim and determined. Once over he will have chuckled. The French will have heard him argue until his knowledge of the language failed, and he will then have been delightfully expressive in English. Some years ago I used to tell him his French beyond a few phrases was execrable and as bad as his singing. I have no doubt that in his triumphal march through Oran the streets will have rung with his wonderful laughter and his pet sayings emphasized with amusing gestures which filled in missing words of a foreign tongue. The tragic end of his wonderful life! I think I can visualize that also. We feel cheated. Will he? I think he will have thought I'm having a run of bad luck. ...if I had lost a brother none could have been more dear to my family.

S.W. Saxton, Paymaster-Commander (Ret.)

Commander Cromwell Varley, DSO, RN, commanded submarines in the First World War. Between the wars, he developed variations of midget submarines. He called on his longtime friend Fritz Peters to produce specialized pumps for the tiny vessels. With his partner Bell, Varley was in command of the Varbel base in the Clyde in Scotland for midget subs.

NAVAL COLLEAGUE CROMWELL VARLEY TO BERTHA JUNE 14, 1943

Dear Mrs. Peters,

I have been waiting to write to you until I was able to get as much information about his gallant and characteristic actions in the attack on Oran, as I could.

It was a desperate adventure against appalling odds and it was only Fritz's grim determination and heroism against these odds which enabled the Walney (his ship) to be berthed alongside the jetty; for he had to run the gauntlet of eight shore batteries and eight warships over a distance of a mile and a half.

He had to secure the lines fore and aft himself as the casualties in his ship were so great.

When he got ashore a man with a tommy gun opened fire on him but he dealt with him and then boarded the flagship where he had an argument with the French admiral who eventually put him in prison. Next morning Oran capitulated and Fritz was carried through the streets and cheered.[i]

In the action he was wounded in the shoulder and blown off the bridge ladder by a shell burst — but he was not badly wounded. His death in the aeroplane crash was instantaneous for she crashed at speed.[ii]

I am sure you know how much I sympathize with you and he is a great loss to me also. My wife and I have asked that the American DSC and the VC should be presented to you in Canada and this has been agreed to.

Cromwell Varley

i. Actually, the Oran surrender was two days later on November 10, 1942.
ii. Varley was mistaken, as Fritz was alive after the crash.

Bertha later received a letter and several photos from a lady in Kent who said she was a special friend of Fritz's. This was the only information on a girlfriend in all the material forthcoming on his life, though he was known to be a hit with ladies of the China Station before the First World War.

GIRLFRIEND DOROTHY BURGESS TO BERTHA   OCTOBER 12, 1944

13 Ethelbert Road, Bromley, Kent

Dear Mrs. Peters

...After much thought and deliberation I have decided to take my courage in both hands and write to you regarding your son in the Royal Navy. We met, Captain Peters and I, at the White Horse Hotel, Haslemere, Surrey, in 1941, where I was then living temporarily on account of its nearness to the firm I then worked for.

At times such as this, during a war, away from one's own home, a certain feeling of loneliness is bound to creep in, and I was no exception to this rule. I had lost my Cavalier some six years before in a sanatorium up in Gloucestershire, and the absence of his companionship and under-standing was affecting me intensely.

With Captain Peters' arrival the dying embers of a 20 years friend-ship was rekindled, and the flame I have since found is very difficult to extinguish. In the ensuing years I must confess I have suffered much, with many bitter disappointments, but I still continue to hold the greatest respect and admiration for your son and a desire to show in some small way my gratitude for what he did for me.

I wrote several letters to him at Portsmouth but although they were never acknowledged I feel certain they would have been, had they ever reached him.

Then last month like a bolt from the blue I had returned to me by the Admiralty ...a small gift I had sent him, in which was enclosed a typewritten note to the effect that Capt. Peters was missing and presumed to have lost his life whilst on Active Service. I immediately wrote to the Admiralty for further details and received an exceedingly kind letter from the Secretary explaining Capt. Peters was presumed to have lost his life in November 1942 when an aircraft in which he was returning from North Africa crashed at Plymouth, South Devon. Again I wrote asking for the name of any relative or friend of his I could get in touch with, and they sent me your name as next of kin.

Mrs. Peters, I cannot say what a great shock this news was to me, nor how proud I am to have met your son, and to realize he holds the added distinction of V.C. to his honours of the last war.

You his mother must have even greater pride over his achievements, and I grieve for you if what we have been told is true. But somehow, I like to think Captain Peters is still with us, and I buoy myself with this hope.

...With the very kindest of thoughts and trusting you have kept safe and well in whatever country you are living during these terrible war years, and that the new year may bring us peace again.

Yours very sincerely, (Miss) Dorothy Burgess
13 Ethelbert Road, Bromley, Kent

On February 2, 1944, a presentation party from the U.S. Army base in Edmonton arrived in Nelson to present Fritz's U.S. DSC medal post-humously to Bertha Peters at the Dewdney residence. The ceremonial party included a brass band and officers led by Col. Dusenbury representing President Roosevelt and Gen. Eisenhower. Bertha was overwhelmed by the event, particularly as the Victoria Cross medal had arrived in the mail a few months before without even a thoughtful covering letter. She was perplexed that her beloved Britain would be so offhand in presenting the highest honour of the Empire, while the nation she disliked below the border was so thoughtful and respectful.

Bertha in 1944 at official presentation of U.S. DSC to her as Fritz's next of kin.

Below, Saxton writes to Bertha after making inquiries about Fritz in the period after his release from the Oran prison and before the fatal flight to England.

SAXTON TO BERTHA   JANUARY 29, 1945

Dear Mrs. Peters

...I have heard no further details of any great interest to you but I can again assure you that he [Fritz] was happy before he left. At Gibraltar he stayed with the Governor I believe or the Admiral of the Port. I believe he has since been relieved. A fortnight ago in London I met an American attached to our navy who might have gone in with FTP but his ship went to Algiers so he could give me no further details of the operation. It seems, however, there were survivors, one a doctor but so far I have not been able to contact him. He was also wounded, I believe. The American officer states that it was the bravest deed of the war with little chance of survival. He was interested to hear that President Roosevelt had deputed high officers to present you with his great honour. My attempt to obtain a case for all his medals has produced nothing so far. It seems there are none on the market and of course none are being made.

...I do so hope the photograph reaches you safely as it should bring you some comfort as it is a nice happy one of FTP. It was taken after we had given a naval dinner at Kumasi. ...FTP was popular with everyone and no party was complete without him. ...He was always ready for a scrap or a roughhouse but he never lost his temper... It was a happy evening and we stayed with him that weekend.

Swain Saxton

On January 2, 1945, British Admiral Bertram Ramsay, who Fritz worked closely with in naval intelligence and when Ramsay was in charge of naval planning for Operation Torch, died when the plane flying him to a conference in Brussels crashed on takeoff at Paris. Fritz was certainly not alone in losing his life in an air crash in wartime outside of action with the enemy. King George VI's brother, the Duke of Kent, died in 1942 when the Short Sunderland flying boat in which he was a passenger crashed into a hillside in Scotland en route to Iceland.

TWO OTHER NELSON VCS

For the Dewdney family, the last days of the Second World War would see another spectacular deed of heroism by someone they knew well. Serving in the Fleet Air Arm, Lt. Hammy Gray in his Corsair plane dramatically attacked and sank a Japanese warship in Onagawa Bay in northern Japan on August 9, 1945. The feat claimed his life but earned a posthumous VC, the last to be awarded to a Canadian. Like Fritz, he was a multiple recipient of awards for valour, previously earning a Mention in Dispatches and British Distinguished Service Cross. Hammy's parents in Nelson, B.C., were invited to a ceremony in Ottawa in February 1946, where the Governor General presented the VC medal to his mother.[11]

Remarkably, all three of Canada's naval VC recipients had a close connection with the small mountain community of Nelson located 400 miles inland from the Pacific Coast. Among the neighbours of the Dewdneys and Grays in Nelson in the 1930s was Lt.-Cdr. (Ret.) Rowland Bourke, VC, DSO, RNVR, who ran a fruit farm at Crescent Bay near Nelson before the First World War. Serving in the Royal Navy, Bourke received the DSO and VC for courageous rescues by his motor launch of commandos in the British attacks in early 1918 on the ports of Ostend and Zeebrugge to prevent moored German subs from escaping to sea. The Ostend raid failed but Zeebrugge was partly successful and heralded as a major victory for Britain at a time when good news from the war was rare.[12]

Bourke left Nelson in 1932 for Victoria where he served with the Royal Canadian Navy in the Second World War. His VC and DSO within a period of three weeks is among the greatest individual Canadian military achievements.

NELSON MOUNTAIN NAMED AFTER FRITZ

In March 1946, a previously unnamed mountain west of Nelson was named in honour of Fritz Peters, even though he never lived in Nelson and just passed through the city on one occasion in 1913. The naming was essentially an afterthought, as the Nelson Board of Trade was looking into options for honouring local VC hero Hammy Gray. They ended up naming a spectacular glacier in Kokanee Glacier Provincial Park as Grays Peak after Hammy and his brother Jack Gray, who died in 1942 serving with the Royal Canadian Air Force. At the same time, a smaller, average-looking mountain of the Selkirk Range on the west edge of Nelson was named Mount Peters. While not intended by the nominators, the low profile of the mountain was in keeping with Fritz's modesty and selflessness.

Bertha Peters died in Nelson in July 1946 at age 84, crippled for the last decade of her life, but still sharp as ever mentally. Her life had spanned the breadth of Canadian history, from meeting the Canadian Fathers of Confederation at her home as a toddler, through six years as a Maritime premier's wife, a decade amongst the leaders of Victoria, B.C., society, five years in frontier Prince Rupert and then three decades in small West Kootenay communities, including two world wars that took the lives of three of her sons. She had virtually no money in her old age and was dependent on her daughter's family for room and board. She tried to earn income writing short stories and novels, but her submissions in the 1920s and 1930s were rejected by publishers.

After Ted Dewdney's death in 1952, his widow Helen came to live with her daughter Dee Dee McBride's family in Nelson.

VICTORIA CROSS CENTENARY IN 1956

In June 1956, Helen Dewdney represented her late brother at the Victoria Cross 100th anniversary events in England. While Helen was proud of Fritz's record of bravery and enjoyed visiting historic venues such as Windsor Castle, she found many of the VC centenary events painful because the marches and music reminded her of the terrible days of the First World War when she lost brothers Jack and Gerald. More than anything else, she detested the song *It's a Long Way to Tipperary* because of bad memories it triggered.

The May 12, 1962, edition of the *Victor* comic books in Britain had a 16-panel comic of Capt. Peters' exploits in Oran harbour, including the dramatic ramming through the boom, surviving point blank shelling of the *Walney* bridge, exchange of fire with French warships, heroic actions to land troops on French ships, and ending with Fritz's release from prison and triumphant parade through the streets of Oran.

In January 1963, Kim Philby avoided pursuers in the Middle East and next showed up in the Soviet Union, for whom he had been a spy since the 1930s. Fritz was among many fooled by Philby, but at least in their time working together at Brickendonbury they were on the same side against Hitler.

The sad life of Fritz's brother Noel, who suffered from abuse and exclusion because of his moderate, though noticeable, mental disability, ended with his death at age 69 at Shaughnessy Veterans Hospital in Vancouver in 1964. The family's last record of contact with him was notification of his mother's death in 1946. He apparently lived on the fringes of society in Vancouver. None of Helen's children or grandchildren ever met Noel. All that was stated in his death notice in the *Vancouver Sun* newspaper was that he had been a soldier in the First World War.

Helen brought the Peters family letters with her when she moved with daughter Dee Dee's family to nearby Trail, B.C., in 1969. Unlike her mother Bertha and brother Fritz, she actually liked the United States, enjoying extended visits to her daughter Eve Fingland's family in California every winter until her death at age 89 in Trail in 1976.

SUNDERLAND RECOVERY

In the summer of 1985, Neil Griffin, a Plymouth recreational diver, spotted wreckage about 60 feet deep in Plymouth Sound while diving. After recovering pieces of fuselage and a propeller with markings identifying it as the Sunderland flying boat with an Australian crew that crashed 43 years before, he contacted the Royal Australian Air Force who were keenly interested in the find.[13]

On May 29, 1987, the propeller went on display at the RAAF Museum at Bull Creek near Perth, Australia, to commemorate a dramatic event in the RAAF's history. Special guests on hand for the opening of the exhibit included the pilot of the fateful flight, Wynton Thorpe, and flight engineer Jack Horgan, who met for the first time in more than 40 years.[14]

In 1993, Fritz's Victoria Cross medal was purchased at auction by Lord Michael Ashcroft, who subsequently amassed a collection of more than a tenth of all VCs ever awarded. Helen's children decided to sell the medal to avoid potential disputes when it was inherited by the next generation.

There was also concern about theft, as some VC medals — including that of Lt. Edward Bellew, who won his VC for the same St. Julien action in which Pte. Jack Peters of the same battalion died — were stolen and never recovered.

On July 12, 2008, Wynton Thorpe, who was probably the last person to see Fritz alive, died in Australia two weeks before his 88th birthday. His family donated his life preserver from the evening of the Sunderland crash to the Australian War Memorial (AWM).[15]

VC MEDAL ON DISPLAY AT IMPERIAL WAR MUSEUM

In November 2010, Fritz's VC medal along with others in the Ashcroft collection went on display in the new Lord Ashcroft Gallery in the Imperial War Museum (IWM) in London, along with 46 VC medals held by the IWM. The gallery was financed by a donation of five million pounds by Lord Ashcroft. In addition to Fritz's VC, the gallery has his DSO medal, DSC and bar, 1914 – 15 Star, and the U.S. DSC medal, as well as display panels and slides detailing his achievements.

There have been several memorial displays honouring Fritz in Charlottetown buildings, including a commissioned painting of Fritz. The Royal Canadian Navy installed memorials to him in the training facilities of HMCS *Queen Charlotte*. His photograph is on display in the Legislature Buildings in Victoria along with other British Columbia recipients of the Victoria Cross.

Like his brothers Jack and Gerald, Fritz has no grave or individual memorial. His name is on the Portsmouth Naval Memorial for navy men of all ranks lost at sea. Like many other aspects of his life, what happened to Fritz's body is a mystery. Most likely, hidden from view by the fog and darkness and with life preserver water-logged after an hour in the icy water, his body quietly sank to the bottom of Plymouth Sound, while RAAF men struggled to assist injured crew members until a rescue boat arrived.

Epilogue
Honour, Selflessness, Courage

I hate war as only a soldier who lived it can; only as one who has seen its brutality, its futility, its stupidity.

— Gen. Dwight D. Eisenhower

In the wake of the horrendous Allied casualties in Oran Bay, some critics — particularly in the U.S. — questioned Capt. Peters' judgment and motives in going ahead with the attack in the face of French fire. With his undiplomatic, uncompromising nature and fierce loyalty to his navy and empire, it is not surprising that Americans found Fritz difficult to work with — and vice versa. To this day, British and Canadian writers tend to be much more favourable in their evaluation of Capt. Peters' leadership at Oran than American writers.

Could Operation Reservist have succeeded? Lt. Moseley, a surviving officer on *Walney*, said in his post-mission report to Admiralty he thought the attack could have succeeded if it coincided with the 1:00 a.m. beach landings and thus had the benefit of surprise. He surmised it could even have worked at 3:00 a.m. if modern destroyers were used rather than cutters.[1] Others, like U.S. naval historian Samuel Morison concluded the operation had no chance, given the French attitude at the time.[2]

Fritz's perception of French attitudes may have been skewed by his familiarity and friendships with courageously anti-Nazi Frenchmen who were trainees in the Brickendonbury spy school he commanded early in the war.

With those Frenchmen willing to put their life — and the lives of their family members — at risk of Nazi torture and execution when they returned to France to join the Resistance, Fritz may have found it incomprehensible that the French safely situated at Oran would side with the Nazi puppets at Vichy against the Allies who shared France's traditions of liberty and democracy, and were steadfast allies at the start of the war and a generation before in the Great War.

In *An Army at Dawn*, American writer Rick Atkinson suggests Capt. Peters — described as a "voluble old salt" — went ahead with the attack because "glory was his goal".[3] The assumption was that he was similar to the egotistical, publicity-seeking generals of the day like Patton and Montgomery. However, Fritz's letters and life story show he abhorred self-promotion and managed to avoid reporters throughout his life, until reluctantly putting up with Disher of United Press because his presence on *Walney* was approved by the Americans.

Fritz preferred to keep a low profile and not display his medals in public. While his personal motivation wasn't fame or enrichment, getting back into the fight was extremely important to him. Like his grandfather, Col. John Hamilton Gray, who desperately tried to get back into active duty when the Crimean War broke out soon after his retirement, Fritz hated being on the sidelines when his Empire was at war.

SOMEONE HAD BLUNDER'D . . .

With its horrific outcome, Operation Reservist was viewed by many as a "blunder" like Tennyson's description of the bad decision to proceed with *The Charge of the Light Brigade*. Tennyson wrote the poem immediately upon hearing news of the charge, and it quickly gained widespread popularity with readers, including British soldiers who appreciated the descriptions of the gallantry of their comrades. Soldiers would often recite the poem at camp, and if officers were within earshot they would emphasize the line "someone had blunder'd" as a subtle dig at officers making mistakes.

With the benefit of hindsight, obviously there should have been a back-out plan and surrender plan for the Oran harbour attack if it encountered fierce resistance from French defenders. In the fall of 1942, however, the Germans were still winning the war and Eisenhower's biggest worry was that his soldiers would be too defensive and lack fighting spirit. Planning for fallbacks and surrenders was not a priority. Based on the intelligence available at the time, it was hoped that a pro-Allied revolt by French officers would stop or at least moderate the resistance to the harbour attack. When that fell through, the result was a massacre.

In 1949, in response to a request from the U.S. Army's Historical Division, Maj. Gen. L.L. Lemnitzer described in a letter what happened with the Oran harbour attack based on his memory and a few brief records. As he recalled, the original plan approved by Eisenhower was to carry out the attack as soon as possible after capitulation of French forces in Oran. He said the plan was changed after Capt. Peters was appointed commander, with the assault then scheduled for two hours after the beach landings (H-hour).[4]

The British had substantially different recollections of how the plan came together. Not surprisingly, in post-war memoirs Eisenhower, Churchill and Cunningham did not go into detail as to their personal involvement in the failed mission. Having served twice as First Lord of the Admiralty, Churchill was known to take a keener personal interest in naval details than those of the other services.[5] Fritz had mentioned to Commander Joel in October 1942 in Scotland that he was personally briefed by Churchill regarding the top secret, extremely hazardous mission on which he was about to embark. Having spent most of his political career trying to live down a reputation he gained for reckless adventurism, following the failed Dardanelles campaign of 1915, Churchill would not relish being connected to a botched mission resulting in a massacre of Allied forces in Oran harbour. In *The Second World War: The Hinge of Fate*, Churchill describes the "gallant attempt" of Allied forces — including many highly-skilled specialists — under Capt. F.T. Peters to capture the harbour, and the "aircraft disaster" in which Fritz died returning to England.[6]

In retrospect, Operation Reservist suffered from dysfunctional team-work, poor communication and the perils of carrying out a military mission by committee. In relative terms, the mission was a blip in what was otherwise a remarkably successful capture of French North Africa. The conflicts between British and American military leaders were part of the growing pains towards an effective alliance.

So was Capt. Peters reckless? His friend Swain Saxton suggested in 1943 that Fritz could not have survived the hundreds of close calls in his life if he were reckless. Until *Walney*, in three stints of service in the navy over a span of close to 38 years, he never lost a ship from under him. His medals were as much for saving the lives of his crew and for rescues at sea as they were for sinking German submarines.

Still, if Fritz survived the Sunderland crash, he had a lot to answer for. His idea of having Lieut. Paul Duncan dress up like a ridiculous cowboy/ gangster American stereotype for the loudspeaker announcement to the French at Oran was an insult to both the Americans and the French. He was certainly the wrong man to lead a cooperative venture with the Americans. Sadly, Fritz never had a chance to explain his actions, as Churchill was to be the first to receive his full report after his return to England in the flying boat.

To his friends, Fritz was a man of loveable eccentricities. It is tempting to see him as similar in some ways to the fictional character Don Quixote, as both Fritz and the Man of La Mancha harkened back to a bygone era of pure ideals, and embarked on personal quests for adventure. Just as

Don Quixote de La Mancha became obsessed with medieval chivalry after excessive reading of books, Fritz became obsessed with the Victorian Age equivalent. However, the comparison should not go too far because Fritz's letters show that, unlike Don Quixote, at the end of the day Fritz was practical, realistic and certainly of sound mind.

There are lists on web sites of men who Ian Fleming may have been thinking about when he came up with the James Bond character. Fritz Peters isn't on these lists, but he could well be, as he was a fearless, quirky, action-seeking bachelor who served with Fleming in British naval intelligence. His remarkably cool demeanour in high-risk conflict situations was well known, as was his Bond-like interest in plastic explosives and warship technology.

Fritz's letters show he was a proud Canadian, even though he chose to live elsewhere in the Empire during his adult years. As was common in his era, he saw himself as both a Canadian and a Britisher, with no conflict between the two allegiances.

More than anything else, Fritz Peters was an old-fashioned Man of Honour. In his life, he avoided publicity and fame as best he could, and only sought enough money to pay off his lingering debts. To the end, he was true to his personal standards of honour and selflessness. He never backed down in defending the honour of his navy, his country and his Empire. He enjoyed the adrenalin rush of battle and was fearless in taking on opponents. His thoughtful letters show the only things he feared were boredom and missing out on the action.

Does Fritz Peters really rank as 'The Bravest Canadian'? He would be first to deny the presumptuous title. How could anyone be braver than air aces William Barker and Billy Bishop, soldiers Edward Bellew and John MacGregor, naval heroes Rowland Bourke and Hammy Gray, or any of Canada's 87 other Victoria Cross recipients? For that matter, how could anyone be braver than Jack Peters at St. Julien, Gerald Peters at Mount Sorrel, or any of the nearly 110,000 other Canadians who lost their lives fighting for Canada in the last century? While it is hardly fair or accurate to single out one person as 'The Bravest Canadian', Fritz Peters' consistent heroism through two world wars stands out as an amazing record of a remarkable Canadian.

Honour the charge they made!
Honour the Light Brigade,
Noble six hundred!

—"The Charge of the Light Brigade" by
Lord Alfred Tennyson

Mount Peters looms above picturesque Nelson, British Columbia, at top centre. At right is the Nelson landmark known as Pulpit Rock, and at bottom left is the west arm of Kootenay Lake.

Chronology

September 17, 1889
Frederic Thornton Peters is born in Charlottetown, Prince Edward Island, Canada, being the second child of Frederick Peters and Bertha Hamilton Susan Gray.

1895
Student at St. Peters (Anglican) Church school in Charlottetown.

November 4, 1897
His father arrives in Victoria, British Columbia with new law partner Sir Charles Hibbert Tupper and the Tupper family, preparing for the move of the Peters family to Victoria.

Prior to September 1900
Student at small private school under schoolmaster Rev. W.W. Bolton on Belcher Street in Victoria.

1900 – 1901
Student at Bedford Grammar School north of London, England.

1901 – 1904
Student at Cordwalles Preparatory School in Maidenhead, England, including Navy courses.

January 1905
Enters Royal Navy as a cadet.

1905
Joins HMS *Britannia* for training, earning the nickname 'Tramp'.

November 11, 1905
Sister Violet Peters dies in a fireplace accident at the family home in Oak Bay.

May 5, 1906
Goes to sea as a midshipman. Appointed to new battleship HMS *Vengeance*, Channel Fleet.

May 5, 1908
Midshipman on battleship HMS *Duncan*, flagship of Rear Admiral Sir George A. Callaghan, Second-In-Command, Mediterranean.

December 28, 1908
Messina earthquake and tsunami. Fritz assists in the recovery and evacuation, earning Italy's Silver Messina Earthquake Medal.

July 30, 1909
Promoted to Acting Sub-Lieutenant. Studying at Portsmouth. Serves at the Royal Navy's China Station in gunboats.

1910
Studying at Royal Navy College, Greenwich.

April 1911
Joined destroyer HMS *Otter*, China Station, as Sub-Lieutenant.

March 26, 1912
Promoted to Lieutenant. Serves on destroyer HMS *Welland*, Hong Kong (April – October).

June 19, 1912
Sister Helen marries Edgar Edwin Lawrence 'Ted' Dewdney at St. Paul's Anglican Church in Esquimalt, B.C.

February 1, 1913
Ship passenger records show he departs from Yokohama, Japan, to Victoria, B.C., on *Empress of India*.

June 1913
Resigns Navy commission to return to Canada. Tries out a variety of jobs, including service on the Canadian Pacific Railway fleet in the B.C. interior.

August 22, 1914
Rejoins Royal Navy as Lieutenant of destroyer HMS *Meteor*, Devonport.

January 24, 1915
Mentioned in dispatches for actions while serving on *Meteor* during action off Dogger Bank in North Sea.

March 3, 1915
Awarded Distinguished Service Order for valour in Dogger Bank naval battle.

April 24, 1915
Brother Private Jack Peters dies in the vicinity of St. Julien in Second Battle of Ypres. Originally listed as missing, with false information that he was a prisoner of war.

November 22, 1915
Lieutenant in command of destroyer HMS *Greyhound*, Portsmouth.

June 3, 1916
Brother Lieutenant Gerald Peters dies in offensive to re-take Mount Sorrel near Ypres.

July 1916
Visits the headquarters of the 7th Battalion of the Canadian Expeditionary Force at Ypres to learn circumstances of Gerald's death and to arrange for burial.

September 14, 1916
Lieutenant in command of destroyer HMS *Christopher*, Chatham.

December 10, 1916
Cousin Eric Skeffington Poole in the British Army is executed for desertion at Poperinghe, Belgium.

August 8, 1917
HMS *Christopher* picks up survivors of Q Ship HMS *Dunraven* sunk by sub UC-71.

October 31, 1917
Lieutenant in command of destroyer HMS *Polyanthus*, Chatham.

January 26, 1918
Lieutenant in command of destroyer HMS *Cockatrice*, Portsmouth.

March 1918
Wins the Distinguished Service Cross for further service in action.

Spring, 1919
Selected for first course at Staff College at Royal Naval College after the war.

July 29, 1919
Father Frederick Peters dies in Prince Rupert, B.C.

March 26, 1920
Promoted to Lieutenant – Commander. Appointed to staff of Commander-in-Chief Atlantic Fleet on HMS *Queen Elizabeth*.

June 26, 1920
Resigns his commission to return to civilian life.

1920 – 1939
Works in Gold Coast colony, now known as Ghana, including cocoa growing. Regular visits back to England for reunions with naval colleagues. Runs engineering works near Bristol.

December 21, 1924
Ship passenger records show he arrived in Liverpool on *Appam* from a voyage that began in Accra, Gold Coast, and stopped at Lagos, Nigeria.

Sept. 17, 1929
Promoted to rank of Commander in Reserve Navy.

Autumn 1939
Re-enters Royal Navy.

October 1939
Commands HMS *Stanhope* and a group of anti-submarine trawlers.

January 1940
Takes command of HMS *Thirlmere* and the Tenth Anti-Submarine Strike Force, the Orkneys and Shetlands command. Sinks two German subs.

June 1940
Appointed to duty with director of naval intelligence.

July 1940
Became Commandant of spy school at Brickendonbury Hall near Hertford.

July 1940
Awarded a bar to his British DSC, presented by King George VI.

February 1941
Serves with director of Anti-Submarine Warfare division.

April 1941
Appointed Staff Officer (Operations) to Commander-in-Chief Portsmouth.

August 1941
Made acting captain and command of HMS *Tynewald*, an auxiliary anti-aircraft vessel.

August 1942
Selected to plan the capture of Oran harbour in Operation Torch, the Allied invasion of French North Africa.

October 23, 1942
Embarks from training base in Scotland on HMS *Walney* destined for Gibraltar and then Oran.

November 6, 1942
Commands the strike force HMS *Walney* and HMS *Hartland* leaving Gibraltar for Oran, Algeria.

November 8, 1942
Leads the 3:00 a.m. attack on Oran harbour in *Walney*. Breaks through harbour boom and lands *Walney* close to target berth but fails to achieve objectives in face of heavy French fire.

November 10, 1942
Freed at noon by Allied troops. Carried on shoulders as a hero in parade through the streets of Oran.

November 13, 1942
Killed along with four other VIP passengers when the Sunderland flying boat returning him to England crashes in Plymouth Harbour. Still conscious

after the crash, he expires in the water as the pilot tried to tow him to safety.

November 28, 1942
Awarded the American Distinguished Service Cross, highest award offered by Americans to a non-American, for heroism at Oran.

May 18, 1943
Awarded Britain's highest honour, the Victoria Cross, for heroism at Oran.

February 4, 1944
Delegation of U.S. officers and brass band arrive in Nelson, B.C., to officially present the U.S. Distinguished Service Cross medal to Bertha Peters as Fritz's next of kin. The Victoria Cross medal had arrived several months earlier in the mail.

July 30, 1946
Mother Bertha Gray Peters dies at age 84 in Nelson, B.C.

July 1, 1964
Brother Noel Peters dies at Shaughnessy Veterans Hospital in Vancouver.

November 25, 1976
Sister Helen Dewdney dies at Trail, B.C.

Summer 1985
Wreckage of the Sunderland flying boat discovered outside Plymouth Sound by recreational diver Neil Griffin.

May 1987
Recovered propeller of the flying boat put on display at Australian air force museum at Perth, Australia in a ceremony attended by pilot Wynton Thorpe and flight engineer Jack Horgan.

July 12, 2008
Wynton Thorpe, who valiantly spent more than an hour trying to carry Fritz as he swam to safety in Plymouth Sound after the 1942 crash, dies in Australia.

November 12, 2010
Capt. Peters' VC medal and four of his other medals are exhibited with display information among exhibits of more than a hundred VC recipients in the new Lord Ashcroft Gallery at the Imperial War Museum in London, England.

MEDALS OF CAPTAIN FREDERIC THORNTON PETERS

Victoria Cross (VC)
For most conspicuous bravery, or some daring, or pre-eminent act of valour or self-sacrifice, or extreme devotion to duty in the presence of the enemy. Established in 1856 by Queen Victoria. Open to all ranks. Tradition dictates that all ranks salute a Victoria Cross holder. The only award that can be granted for action in which the recipient is killed, other than Mention in Dispatches.

Distinguished Service Order (DSO)
For valour, second only to the Victoria Cross. Rewards individual instances of meritorious or distinguished service in war. Normally given for service under fire. Awarded to officers of all ranks, but more commonly to officers with ranks of major or higher.

Distinguished Service Cross (DSC) and Bar
Third-level award for valour for British naval officers. For gallantry during active operations against the enemy at sea. A bar is awarded for a subsequent DSC.

Mention in Dispatches
Name appears in a report by a superior officer to high command, describing gallant or meritorious action. May be awarded posthumously.

1914 – 15 Star
For service in any theatre of war August 5, 1914 - Dec. 31, 1915.

British War Medal (1914 – 20)
For the conclusion of First World War and further operations up to 1920.

Victory Medal (1914 – 19)
For successful conclusion of First World War.

1939 – 45 Star
For completing six months service overseas.

Atlantic Star
For six months service with Royal Navy afloat in Atlantic, home waters and North Russia.

Africa Star and bar (1940 – 43)
For operations in North Africa.

Defence Medal (1939 – 45)
For three years service at home or six months service overseas.

War Medal (1939 – 45)
For all full-time personnel in Second World War.

Messina Earthquake Commemoration Medal (1908)
For assisting in rescue and recovery after the Messina earthquake in Sicily in 1908.

Distinguished Service Cross (DSC) (USA)
U.S. Army award for valour second only to the Congressional Medal of Honor. For extreme gallantry and risk of life in actual combat with an armed enemy. Highest award that can be bestowed by the United States on a non-American.

Capt. Peters' medals currently displayed at the Imperial War Museum.

From left to right, the VC, DSO, DSC and bar, DSC (U.S.) and 1914-1915 Star.

APPENDIX A
ANCESTRY OF FREDERIC THORNTON PETERS

Fritz's ancestors in the Peters line are believed to have originated in France, migrating through Flanders to Cornwall and Devon in England.[1]

A distant relation, the Puritan Reverend Hugh Peters, was the subject of a substantial portion of the material in the Peters family history file read by Fritz Peters and his siblings. Rev. Peters sailed to America a decade after the *Mayflower* and was a founding governor of Harvard College and a leader of efforts to establish Connecticut as a colony separate from Massachusetts. He returned to England in 1641 to gain support for his causes in America and never came back, as he enthusiastically joined Oliver Cromwell as a senior lieutenant and propagandist in battles against Royalist forces in the English Civil War. In 1660, after Cromwell's death and the Restoration of the monarchy, Hugh courageously refused to admit to a vengeance-seeking mob that Parliament's execution of King Charles I in 1649 was wrong, despite protracted torture and humiliation in a public square before he was drawn and quartered – one of the most painful and gruesome forms of execution ever devised by man.

The first Peters ancestor to settle permanently in North America was Dr. Charles Peters from London. He arrived in New York in 1703 and married Mary Hewlett, whose Dutch ancestors were in the community half a century earlier when it was known as New Amsterdam. By the time of the American Revolution, the Peters were among the leading families of Hempstead, Long Island. Like many residents of New York, the family sided with the King against the rebels.

After the rebels' victory was acknowledged in the Treaty of Paris, Dr. Peters' grandson, lawyer James Peters, led a group of Loyalists to settle in what became Saint John, New Brunswick. James was appointed Justice of the Peace, named Judge of the Inferior Court of Queen's County and served in the New Brunswick House of Assembly, starting a Peters family tradition of lawyers, judges and political service in Canada's Maritime region. In his estate, James Peters' papers included letters from U.S. President George Washington inviting him to return to New York with his property restored, but he chose to stay loyal to Britain.[2]

THE CUNARD CONNECTION

James Peters' son, the Hon. Thomas Horsfield Peters, a prosperous New Brunswick lawyer, was appointed Clerk of the Peace and Deputy Treasurer of the colony and served in the legislative council. His son James Horsfield Peters was born in Saint John, trained in law and settled in Charlottetown, where he married Mary Cunard, eldest daughter of prominent Halifax businessman Samuel Cunard in 1837. It was the second marital connection between the Peters and Cunard families, as four years earlier James' older sister Mary Peters married Samuel's brother Joseph Cunard.[3] From 1838 until his appointment as assistant judge of the Supreme Court in 1848, James Horsfield Peters was lawyer and agent for the Prince Edward Island

interests of his father-in-law Cunard. He then served as a judge in P.E.I. for 43 years.

A man of many talents and interests, Judge Peters was known for his deep concern for the rights of the accused, for agricultural improvements in the island such as crop rotation, and for designing a better and safer iceboat for winter travel to and from the mainland.[4] Despite these achievements, this Renaissance Man of the island never lived down the stories of his early days as a land agent carrying four stylish pistols with him as he knocked on doors collecting rent for the Cunards.

Judge James Horsfield Peters.

AMONG THE FIRST GERMANS IN AMERICA

The Cunard ancestors were among the first Germans to settle in North America – the only significant non-British line in Fritz's roots. Known then as Kunders, they were part of a group of Quakers from Krefield in the Rhine region who settled near today's Philadelphia in the 1680s.[5] Ninety years later, the family was split in its response to the Revolution. Samuel's father Abraham — a successful Pennsylvania shipbuilder who regularly dealt with the Royal Navy in his work — and his brother Robert Cunard stayed loyal to the King, while everyone else in the family sided with the rebels. Abraham met his future wife, Ireland-born Margaret Murphy of South Carolina, during the Loyalist evacuation voyage to Nova Scotia in the spring of 1783 after the rebel colonies gained independence and evicted their adversaries.

Sir Samuel Cunard

Born in Halifax in 1787, their son Samuel would become a giant of international commerce, pioneering the new industry of steam-driven transatlantic passenger service. Though short in stature, he would dominate a room with his energy, charm and eloquence. In 1840, Cunard was greeted as a hero by New Englanders when his first steamship *Britannia* brought mail from Britain to Boston. However, American politicians were aghast to see a foreigner dominating a vital new industry. Congress provided a large subsidy to Edward Knight Collins to establish American dominance in the industry, but Collins' emphasis on speed over safety resulted in numerous well-publicized wrecks, while Cunard maintained leadership in passenger travel through a record of safety and reliability.[6] The Cunard line's stellar record for passenger safety over three-quarters of a century was shattered with the sinking of the liner *RMS Lusitania* by a German torpedo in May 1915.

Cunard was knighted by Queen Victoria in appreciation for the steamships he provided at short notice for transporting troops to the Crimean War. Thus began a Cunard Steamship Lines tradition of seconding passenger ships for Britain's wartime needs, memorably with the *Queen Mary* in camouflage paint carrying up to 15,000 soldiers at a time across the Atlantic in World War Two. In addition to a fleet of more than 40 ships, Sir Samuel Cunard invested widely in the tea business and a variety of other ventures such as forests and farmland in Prince Edward Island.

BROTHERS SUCCEED IN LAW AND POLITICS

James Horsfield Peters and Mary Cunard had six children, including sons Frederick and Arthur who both became lawyers and served as Premier and Attorney General of P.E.I.

Frederick Peters knew his famous grandfather well from Cunard's many visits to Charlottetown, and was inspired by Cunard's success as a risk-taking businessman. His mother Mary was one of nine children of Cunard, most of whom settled in England, so Fred had numerous uncles, aunts and cousins in England on the Cunard side. Sir Samuel's will left each of his daughters 20,000 pounds,[7] enabling Judge Peters' family to live in considerable comfort and security, although not prosperous enough to ensure that the next generation was free of money worries.

Fred was a student at Prince of Wales College in Charlottetown, then King's College in Nova Scotia, and read law in England in the office of Lord Alverstone, who later said Fred Peters was the most brilliant student he ever had.[8] The connection with Lord Alverstone turned out to be a negative for Fred after Alverstone's ruling as an arbitrator in favour of the American side in the Alaska Boundary Dispute in 1903. The outcome was extremely unpopular in Canada, particularly in B.C.

Arthur Peters followed Fred in the same schooling almost step for step, and they became partners in the Charlottetown law firm of Peters, Peters and Ings.

POETS IN THE FAMILY

While the Peters in the Maritimes in that era were best known as lawyers, judges and public officials, Fred's cousins on the Peters side also included well-known Canadian poets Bliss Carman and Sir Charles G.D. Roberts.[9]

There were two significant military connections in the extended family. Fred's sister Carrie's father-in-law was Admiral Henry Wolsey Bayfield of the Royal Navy, a hydrographer who surveyed many of central and eastern Canada's waterways for safe navigation.[10] Bayfield went to sea at age 11 in 1806 and rose to Admiral 61 years later, shortly before retirement in 1867. Many of his surveys were still in use until the onset of global positioning system technology.

Fred's cousin Capt. (later Maj. and then Col.) James Peters, a native of Saint John, N.B., joined the 62nd Fusiliers militia at 17 in 1870 to defend against an anticipated raid by Fenians — Irish-Americans determined to gain independence for their homeland by attacking the British in Canada. In charge of an artillery battery, he was mentioned in dispatches for service in the Riel Rebellion of 1885, when he was also working as a correspondent for the *Quebec Morning Chronicle*. A keen amateur photographer, Capt. James Peters had the distinction of taking the world's first battlefield action photographs, using new camera technology to take photos during the Battle of Fish Creek while on horseback. Previously, war photographs were only taken after battles were over, due to the cumbersome camera equipment of the time.

In 1887, Maj. James Peters commanded a 100-man battery from Quebec that traveled by train across Canada and then by boat to Victoria to be the first permanent force to defend Canada's west coast.[11] When Fred Peters and family from Charlottetown arrived in Victoria in 1897, his cousin Col. James Peters regularly hosted his relations, including tours of warships at the Royal Navy's Pacific Station naval base at Esquimalt, adjacent to Victoria.

TWO COLONELS GRAY

The military heroes of Fritz's ancestry were predominantly on the Gray side, beginning with his great-grandfather Col. Robert Gray, born near Glasgow, Scotland, in 1747 in an area where Gray was a widely-held surname. In autobiographical notes written for his grandchildren, Robert said his parents, Andrew Gray and Jean Gray, lost ownership of their property in Dunbartonshire through a "reverse of fortune" and were paying rent to a distant relation who also happened to be named Robert Gray.[12]

While traditional ways of making a living were in decline, the business of selling and distributing tobacco brought over from America was thriving in and around Glasgow. When young Robert Gray was offered work as a storekeeper and agent in Virginia for the Hamilton family of tobacco merchants, he jumped at the chance. He felt grateful to the Hamiltons the rest of his life, and asked Thomas Hamilton of Overton to be godfather to his youngest son, John Hamilton Gray.[13] This began a family naming tradition that has seen dozens of Robert's descendants over five generations carry Hamilton as a first or middle name, including Fritz Peters' mother, brother, grandfather, uncle, aunt, cousins, nephew and great-nephew.

Living in much-improved circumstances in America, Robert Gray couldn't fathom why many neighbours were chronically dissatisfied and rebellious against the King's authority. Scots in the tobacco business overwhelmingly sided with King George before and during the Revolution. In his memoirs, Robert angrily denounced the "damned Rebels" who torched his business in Norfolk, Virginia.

His response to the revolution was to help raise a regiment to fight against it. He wrote that he was "dangerously wounded, being shot in two places" while leading troops in the bitter battles of the Carolinas, commanding a company in the King's Own Regiment known for the ferocity of its fighting.

"I GLORY IN THE NAME OF TORY"

Col. Robert Gray was taken prisoner on one occasion when men serving under him flipped to support the rebels. Robert wrote that he experienced "barbarous acts" while held by the enemy. This added to a tradition of antagonism towards the United States that would continue in the family for generations, including Robert's granddaughter Bertha Gray and her son Fritz Peters. Robert never wavered from his fervent support of the King. "What assistance I can give shall not be wanting, as I glory in the name of TORY!" he wrote in a letter to a friend in Scotland.[14] After the war, he helped in the settling of fellow Loyalists in modern-day Nova Scotia and New Brunswick, receiving substantial government appointments and land in P.E.I. in appreciation of his service.

In the late 1790s at about age 50, Robert Gray married much-younger Mary Burns, daughter of Lieut. George Burns and Mary Stukeley, and they had six children, the last being John Hamilton Gray in 1811.

THE FAMILY'S MR. WICKHAM

Born in Middlesex, England in 1738, George Burns was noteworthy in Fritz's ancestry in two respects. First, he was an original proprietor — part of the first group to receive land grants after the British took control of Prince Edward Island in the mid-18th century — so Fritz's roots in P.E.I. go back to the beginning of the island's history as a British possession. Secondly, Burns was remembered by descendants as the Black Sheep of the family.

The Gray and Peters children were told of him as an example of how *not* to live their lives. In family history notes written for her grandchildren in the 1890s, Bertha's sister Florence Poole said her father John Hamilton Gray and his brother Robert blamed their grandfather Burns for the painful gout they suffered and supposedly inherited from him. According to Florence, Burns was a "very fast man about town" and a "four-bottle man" who consumed unlimited quantities of port.[15]

Florence said Burns originally received a substantial land grant on the north side of P.E.I. for his service in the honour guard at the coronation of King George III. Like the Wickham character in Jane Austen's *Pride and Prejudice* novel of the same era, Burns raised his station in life by eloping with the daughter of a more prosperous family. Mary — daughter of Squire Adelard of the prominent Stukeleys of Huntingtonshire — was 18 and visiting Bath when the 31-year-old Lieut. Burns swept her off her feet, marrying her in London in 1766. Burns squandered the wealth he gained from inheritances, land grants and government appointments, and left P.E.I. for Ireland in the 1790s, heavily in debt and with a cloud over his head, dying in Dublin in 1801. Marriage was his one area of success, as his two daughters also married well — Mary Burns to Robert Gray when he was prospering as Treasurer and Chief Justice of P.E.I., and Phoebe Burns to Gray's former commander in the Revolutionary War, Gen. Edmund

Fanning, who served as Governor of the P.E.I. colony for 15 years. As a young man, John Hamilton Gray visited the Stukeleys in England and found there was still resentment against his grandfather Burns for stealing away their 'Molly', as Mary was called within her family.[16]

AN UNLIKELY POLITICIAN AND FATHER OF CONFEDERATION

John Hamilton Gray stands out in island history as the host of the famous Charlottetown Conference of 1864 and one of P.E.I.'s Fathers of Confederation, but his family knew him as a military man who disliked politics. Historian David Weale noted that when John Hamilton Gray was born in 1811, "the Gray family was solidly within the ruling

John Hamilton Gray.

upper class of the island and his career, both as soldier and as politician was to a great extent predetermined by family tradition."[17]

Growing up in Charlottetown, Gray went to Britain at age 19 to become an officer in the Dragoon Guards, made possible through his father's purchase of the appointment. His first two marriages were while serving in India. At 27, he married the widow Fanny Sewell Chaumier who died within a year in childbirth.[18] Then, about three years later, he married Susan Ellen Bartley Pennefather, with whom he had five daughters and no sons. When Gray served as aide-de-camp for the Prince of Wales' visit to P.E.I. in 1860, he mentioned to the future King Edward VII that he had daughters born in each of the four quadrants of the world: Harriet in a troop ship en route to India, Margaret in South Africa, Florence in England and Mary in Charlottetown. Several years later, the Prince was chatting in England with Gen. Pennefather about the Prince's visit to P.E.I. The Prince said he met an interesting fellow who had daughters born in each quarter of the globe. Pennefather said "That was my son-in-law, and one of his daughters is visiting me now!"

Bertha was the baby of the family, with sister Mary (known as Mim in the family) two years older and three much older sisters. Bertha rarely saw Harriet, 19 years her senior, because her parents sent Harriet as a teen-ager to Aldershot, England to live with and look after her elderly Pennefather grandparents. Margaret, 16 years older than Bertha, helped raise her younger sisters after their mother Susan died in 1866. Though just four when Susan died, Bertha had many memories of her, referring to her in chats with her children and grandchildren as "my dear little mama".

After Margaret's marriage to P.E.I. shipbuilder Artemus Lord in 1869, the 'mother' role at Inkerman House went to Florence, 14 years older than Bertha. Meanwhile, the widower John Hamilton Gray married Sarah Caroline Cambridge, with whom he had three more children, though only Arthur Cavendish Hamilton Gray survived past childhood. Florence married prominent mining engineer Henry Skeffington Poole in 1876, settling in Stellarton, Nova Scotia, for about 25 years before moving to England. In 1887, Mim married William Abbott, son of Canadian Prime Minister Sir John Abbott, and their Montreal residence would later be a regular stop for members of the Peters family travelling to or returning from England.

WIDOW MARRIES SIR JOHN PENNEFATHER

Bertha's mother Susan was the daughter of Lt. William Bartley of County Monaghan and Margaret Carr of Dublin, both families of Protestant, Anglo-Irish stock. Susan was born in about 1825 in Jamaica where her father was stationed with Britain's 22nd Regiment. As was common among soldiers abroad in that era, Bartley became ill and died in Jamaica. A year later, his commanding officer, Maj. Sir John Lysaght Pennefather of Anglo-Irish aristocracy, married Margaret and she became Lady Pennefather — a title cherished by her and the next four generations of descendants, including her granddaughter Bertha. Gen. Pennefather preferred that the step-relationship with Susan not be known in the community. She only learned Pennefather wasn't her biological father when told just before marrying 31-year-old John Hamilton Gray when she was 17. Susan was popular in Charlottetown, known for her efforts helping the poor.

At the outbreak of the Crimean War between Russia and Britain and her allies in 1854, John Hamilton Gray — who had retired to Charlottetown the previous year after a full 21-year term in the army with no major wars — sold his Spring Park estate and rushed to the Crimea hoping to regain his old position. He was bitterly disappointed to find the Army would not take him back. Then he was thrilled when his father-in-law Pennefather — now holding the rank of General and known for his aggressive tactics in battle — took him on as a staff assistant. However, by the time Gray got to the front the war was over. While in the Crimea, he heard much of Pennefather's spectacular success at the Battle of Inkerman, 11 days after the disastrous charge at Balaclava that became famous as *The Charge of the Light Brigade*. Pennefather, in command of 2,700 troops of the Second Division who defeated 15,300 Russians, inspired his men by personally leading them in an attack through heavy fog which saw his horse killed from under him. He was described by Gen. Sir Edward Hamley in War in the Crimea as:

> "A very power in himself. Even when his radiant countenance could not be seen there was comfort in the sound of his voice and the 'grand old boy's' favourite oath roaring cheerfully through the smoke."[19]

This wasn't Pennefather's first spectacular success in battle against a more numerous opponent. Eleven years earlier, in the Battle of Meanee in India, his force of 500 Irishmen defeated 30,000 Indians.

When Gray returned to P.E.I., he built a new estate and named it Inkerman House in honour of his father-in-law's famous battle. Gray personally planted trees along his entrance, known as Inkerman Way to represent the order of battle at Inkerman, with linden trees precisely 40 feet apart on one side representing the Russians and a mixture of white birch, beech, mountain ash and poplars on the other side representing the British and French.[20]

COL. GRAY WON A DUEL

Fritz often heard stories from his mother and her sisters of his grandfather Gray as a military hero as well as a Father of Confederation. Florence Poole wrote of her father leading a charge with three mounted policemen to 'spike' an enemy gun emplacement in South Africa in the mid-1840s.[21] She said the action would have earned him a Victoria Cross if the medal was available at the time (the VC was established in 1856 by Queen Victoria).

In John Hamilton Gray's time, duelling to settle disputes was not only legal, it was encouraged. As a new officer in the Black Horse of the Dragoons, he was issued a pair of duelling pistols with which to uphold the honour of the regiment. Florence said her father participated in at least one duel, where he wasn't hit but "winged his man".[22] Returning to Charlottetown from the Crimea, Gray took charge of the island's militia.

ENTHUSIASTIC SUPPORTER OF CONFEDERATION

Gray became involved in government when he believed it was his duty as a man of prominence. He began a term as Premier of P.E.I. in 1863, not realizing that his time in office would involve a significant role in the founding of Canada. He was initially keen on the idea of a Maritime Union, and became even more enthusiastic upon hearing the proposal from leaders of Upper and Lower Canada for a self-governing union of the British colonies across the continent.

When participants in the Charlottetown Conference met for the first time on September 1, 1864, their first decision was to elect their host Premier John Hamilton Gray as conference chairman. Over the next couple of days, the proposal from leaders of Upper and Lower Canada for a united Canada from sea to sea was methodically presented to curious delegates from the Maritime colonies.

Enthusiasm for confederation did not take hold until Saturday, September 3, 1864, after adjournment of the day's conference proceedings. Delegates enjoyed a late afternoon dinner hosted by the delegation from Upper and Lower Canada on the government steamer *Queen Victoria* in Charlottetown harbour. Toasts and congratulations were offered back and forth, plenty of champagne, claret and sherry consumed, and it became evident that an agreement was much more likely than before the dinner.[23]

The spirit of goodwill and friendliness travelled with the 23 gentlemen as they moved on to Inkerman House for an after-dinner party hosted by Gray. As the next day was Sunday and there would be no conference business on the Sabbath, the merriment continued well into the evening. Upper Canada delegate and Toronto *Globe* editor George Brown wrote, "Col. Gray gave a grand dinner party at his beautiful mansion".[24]

CLOSE ENCOUNTERS WITH THE TUPPERS

The delegates decided to get together again a month later at Quebec City to further their discussions towards a new self-governing nation. It was en route to the Quebec Conference in October that Bertha's family had one of its many encounters over the years with the Tupper family. The boat transporting Nova Scotia Premier Dr. Charles Tupper, Lady Tupper and their daughter Emma to the conference stopped at Charlottetown to pick up P.E.I. delegates. The Tuppers encountered Margaret Gray at Inkerman House and talked her father into taking her along to the conference. She came home to her sisters raving about the wonderful dinners and balls with exquisitely dressed ladies and gentlemen. By the 1930s, Margaret, who died in Charlottetown at 96 in 1941, was the last living attendee of the Quebec Conference.[25]

As a military man, Gray was well aware of the danger P.E.I. and other British colonies faced in the mid-1860s from hundreds of thousands of battle-hardened troops below the border, as the North was about to defeat the South in the U.S. Civil War, and angry at Britain for siding with the South, albeit modestly, because Britain opposed slavery.

In addition to increased security, Gray saw a united Canada as a means to strengthen the island's hand in dealings with Britain. He was embarrassed when he enthusiastically supported Confederation, only to find a majority of his colleagues in the island government backed off and were opposed. Along with concern about his wife Susan's illness, this led to Gray's resignation as Premier, exit from island politics and return to leading the island's militia as Adjutant General.

After Gray's death in 1887, the Charlottetown newspaper, *The Patriot*, described him succinctly as "a strict disciplinarian and punctual to a fault". Bertha told her grandchildren that her famous father was a formidable figure to her as a child — "a very stern man, perhaps cruel, but strong."[26]

Bertha went by several names in her life. She was registered as Roberta Hamilton Susan Gray, but known as Bertha in the community, Bertie or 'B' to her sisters, Zarig to her children and Dally to her grandchildren. She enjoyed introducing herself as a Daughter of Confederation, inheriting a playful, eccentric nature and tendency to strident opinions from her father, which she in turn passed on to her son Fritz. Her reverence for the British Empire, her old-fashioned ideas and wariness towards the United States are understandable in light of the fact she was only two generations away from the Revolutionary War. In contrast, her husband Fred, who was 10 years older, was three generations away. Her generations were long in years because her father was 51 years old when she was born, and his father Robert was 64 when John Hamilton Gray was born.

TWO LEADING P.E.I. FAMILIES UNITED IN MARRIAGE

The wedding of Bertha Gray and Fred Peters on October 19, 1886, was a highlight of the closely-knit island social scene, bringing together families whose paths crossed many times in the past. Even before Bertha was born, Fred's sister Carrie Peters was Margaret Gray's best friend. The Grays also knew and visited the Cunards, and there was much travel by family members back and forth across the Atlantic.[27] While both families were solidly situated in the island establishment, the Peters were better off financially thanks to the Cunard inheritance. The 1881 census shows there were six servants residing with the Peters at Sidmount House, and four servants with the Grays at Inkerman House.

Like her father and grandfather, Bertha was a voracious reader with firm opinions, such as the superiority of English private schools. As a result, she insisted her children attend private schools in England even when the family could not afford it.

When Bertha's husband Fred was buried at historic Ross Bay Cemetery in Victoria in 1919, someone noted that his gravesite was located about 100 feet from that of a Father of Confederation named John Hamilton Gray — but it wasn't Bertha's father. By great coincidence, there were two unrelated Fathers of Confederation named John Hamilton Gray, one in New Brunswick and one in P.E.I. The New Brunswick Gray spent his latter years in Victoria and was buried at Ross Bay. Bertha's father rests in Sherwood cemetery in Charlottetown.

APPENDIX B
ADDITIONAL LETTERS

Dear Mother:

. . . I suppose by the time you get this you will have read all about the naval battle[i] in which Fritz figured when the Meteor had a shell put through her killing four and wounding one, putting her out of action. It must have been pretty exciting while it lasted . . . . If I come across any good account in the paper written by a Meteor man I'll send it to you. The trouble is that we often don't get any papers in this wilderness.

. . . If we do go to the front right away, of course, you needn't worry about me because I don't intend to put my head up above the trench to shoot the Germans. Me for where the earth is thickest and highest.

Jack

i. This was the Battle of Dogger Bank in the North Sea in January 1915, for which Fritz was mentioned in dispatches and later received the Distinguished Service Order medal for heroism on the destroyer HMS *Meteor*.

160

Lark Hill Camp[i]
Dear Mother,

    . . . The King and Kitchener[ii] together with a small army of generals and a stray admiral reviewed us yesterday. This was our farewell review before going to France. All the men are reviewed by the King before they go out. Colonel McHarg[iii] reminded me very much of poor old Captain Stork[iv] when he said to us "Boys, you've done well".
    . . . We expect to go to France any day now. Ammunition has been served out to us. I think we are going to take the Ross Rifle[v] to the front with us after all . . . I wrote to Fritz for an account of the battle but haven't received any answer so far. I wish I could have seen him before I left. I'll be gone before Gerald arrives.
    I suppose Gerald has gone by now and you are feeling low. I hope you'll be able to make it in the summer. Just about the time when I am invalided back to England.

Jack

i.   In Salisbury Plain in England where the Canadian First Contingent trained in rain and mud in the worst winter weather in memory.

ii. King George V and Britain's Minister of War, Lord Horatio Kitchener, whose stern likeness was on recruitment posters throughout the British Empire.

iii. Col. William Hart-McHarg (1869–1915), a two-time Canadian champion sharpshooter, was in command of the 7th B.C. Duke of Connaught's Battalion. Jack's brother-in-law Ted Dewdney knew him in Rossland, B.C., at the turn of the century when they were both in the local Rocky Mountain Rangers militia. Hart-McHarg did research work for the Alaska Boundary Commission at the same time as Fred Peters, and was interviewed by Vancouver's Province newspaper after the arbitration decision. In the Second Battle of Ypres, he was shot when spotted by German soldiers reconnoitring the new battle lines on April 23, 1915. He was able to crawl back to safety but died the next day from his wounds.

iv. Originally from Bolton, Ontario, Alfred Stork was the city of Prince Rupert's first mayor. He was commanding officer of the first military organization in the city, the Earl Grey's Own Rifles, which Jack, Gerald and Noel Peters joined as cadets.

v. Canada's Defence and Militia Minister Sam Hughes insisted that Canadian soldiers use the Canadian-made Ross Rifle, against the wishes of British generals and Canadian soldiers who found the rifle jammed when hot after rapid firing, or if wet and muddy.

PRIVATE JACK PETERS TO HIS COUSIN EVELYN POOLE   APRIL 13, 1915

Dear Evelyn,

> *. . . Our rest is over now for we leave for the firing line tomorrow, and from all reports we may really be up against something this time. It's been quite like Salisbury Plain again, what with Company drill and bayonet exercises . . .*

Your affectionate cousin,

Jack Peters[i]

i. This was the last letter from Jack, as he died on Saturday, April 24, 1915, in the 2nd Battle of Ypres when Canadian troops made a courageous stand with no protective masks against a German attack that used poison chlorine gas. Four Victoria Crosses were awarded to Canadians in the battle, including Lieut. Edward Bellew of Jack's 7th Battalion. John McCrae, a surgeon in charge of a field hospital, wrote "*In Flanders Fields*" on May 3, 1915, inspired by the death of a close friend in the same battle.

PRIVATE GERALD PETERS TO HIS MOTHER BERTHA   APRIL 17, 1915

Khaki Club[i]

My Dearest Beetle,

> *. . . Strange that poor Noel should be the first to suffer out of our family in this cause.[ii] I do hope he soon gets better. Thank Heavens none of us drink or smoke. Here is where that will count . . .*

[rest of letter missing]

i. Soldier recreation centre in Montreal.

ii. Noel had a serious nervous breakdown, likely a result of bullying he received due to his noticeable mental disability. It caused
Bertha to cancel the arrangements for her trip to England at
the last minute.

PTE. GERALD PETERS TO HIS SISTER HELEN   JULY 17, 1915

Sandling Hutments[i]

My Dearest Ode Hagen,[ii]

*I should have written before, but I waited to hear more news of Jack.[iii]
I suppose you know he was reported missing since April 25th. Aunt Flor-
ence told me this in her first letter. Yesterday she wrote saying that Aunt
Helen has found out through some friends of hers in Switzerland that
Jack is a prisoner in Hanover.[iv] It is a great relief to hear he is still alive.
I was afraid he had been killed in the fighting around Ypres Apr 24 – 27.
About 350 officers and men of the 7th were captured with him.*

*I got a cheery letter from Fritz yesterday. He hadn't heard Jack was
a prisoner for certain and said that after all, one of us three at least was
bound to be killed. He doesn't expect to get any leave before August so I
won't be able to see him until then.*

*. . . I only hope if I am wounded it will be in some civilized part and
not in the stomach etc. where you can't ever tell people about it.*

[rest of letter missing]

i. Canadian barracks in Kent in southeast England.

ii. Family nickname for sister Helen.

iii. Jack was listed as missing in the 2nd Battle of Ypres, as the
Germans took over the town of St. Julien his battalion was
protecting, and many prisoners were taken. His body was never
recovered, and the manner of his death was never determined.
Most deaths in the battle were from the huge number of artillery shells launched by both sides.

iv. The speculation that he was a prisoner of war in Hanover
proved to be completely wrong.

LIEUT. GERALD PETERS TO HIS SISTER HELEN   FEBRUARY 13, 1916

My Dearest Ode Hagen,

No doubt Mother has told you already about my amazing luck. The right amount of pull has succeeded in getting me a commission[i] and I am back in dear old England and out of that Blasted Bloody Belgium. You can't imagine how glorious it is to be back. It was simply miserable over there.

. . . My pay will be pretty good — $60 a month and $18 allowance while in England. So I will be able to let Mother have quite a bit.

. . . I rather dread going back as an officer. It is a real responsibility — even a junior officer — as he has control of a platoon, about 50 men, and perhaps a big extent of trench. Fancy having to take out wiring parties to within 40 yards of the Germans and work for three hours in the open. It's bad enough to be on these parties, let alone commanding them . . . . If you ever hear a man say he wants to get back to the firing line again, you can tell him he is a darned liar.

Your loving,

Zarig

i.   His service file shows that he was accepted into Officer Training on Feb. 12, 1916.

LIEUT. GERALD PETERS TO HIS MOTHER BERTHA   MAY 24, 1916

Belgium

My dearest Zarig,

. . . I can't tell you how splendid this battalion is. The spirit of all the officers and men is wonderful . . . . Harris seemed really delighted I had come, and introduced me to the others as one of his "oldest chums". Rather decent of him. He talked a lot of poor old Jack. He said he had never met a man so cheerful and optimistic always . . . It will reassure you to hear that we are going in to a pretty civilized part of the line. The method in the battalion is to give the Germans complete hell the first time in a trench, and then secure the upper hand at once. The men seem to be beyond compare.

Your loving

Zarig

LIEUT. GERALD PETERS TO HIS MOTHER BERTHA   MAY 31, 1916

My Dearest Zarig

. . . We are behind the lines in reserve, and by the time you get this we will probably be still farther back and I don't think we will be in the trenches again for a month . . .

Your loving

Gerald[i]

i.   This was the last communication from Gerald before he died in the Canadian attack on Mount Sorrel in the Ypres Salient on June 3, 1916.

SGT. MAJOR DAWSON TO FRED PETERS   CIRCA AUGUST 1916

Dear Sir:

I have just got your address, and I thought I should like to let you know your son died just like a hero.

. . . We got orders to advance from our present front line, which was really our old support line, as the Huns were occupying our front trench. Well, Sir, we had about 700 yards to go, and the rain of machine gun bullets was just like hail stones, but the boys just went over to their death with a mighty cheer. I saw Gerald drop, and the last words I heard him say were "Keep on boys, right after them". I shall always remember him, he was the coolest boy I think I have ever seen, and he seemed so young. He dropped just about 60 yards outside our parapet, and that is the last I saw of him. The boys were just dropping like flies, the line was very thin, and by the time we got halfway we had 75% casualties . . . I know how it must have upset you all, over Gerald's death, but I am glad I can console you a little with the story of how he died, as game as a lion and as gentle as a lamb. His life was short but, by God, he was a man. It quite upset me when I heard he was killed.

Coy. Sgt. Major Dawson, C.F.
7th Batt., c/o Army P.O., London. Moore Bks Hospital.

FRITZ TO HIS MOTHER BERTHA   CIRCA NOVEMBER 1916

. . . I do not often see the Brackenburys living at Hampstead, which is really quite easy I suppose to get at from London, but I am not in love with the tube and a taxi costs the half of one's princely fortune . . .

. . . The really annoying part is I know I don't look old enough. I think I shall grow a beard and mustache.

No, on second thought, I will not. I should never dare tackle a poached egg — a weakness, yes a distinct weakness — again.

Yours,
Fritz[i]

i.   This letter was ripped in half, with one of the sections missing.

FRITZ TO HIS MOTHER BERTHA   SEPTEMBER 22, 1917

My Dear Mother,

Many thanks for your letter, which I received not long ago, the first for some months. It is always an excellent maxim to attack first, hence my remark concerning your letter. I fear my own correspondence is none too brilliant, but then it never has been nor will it ever be.

I suppose you are now at Prince Rupert, and I trust that Father is well and going as strong as ever. How are the Clements? Please give them my regards.

It is now three weeks since I left the old Christopher, and I am still without a ship – exceptional happening in these days. The leave is very acceptable and I spent a perfect 10 days of it at Hodsock and managed to kill a few partridges. The partridge is a good bird, but I must admit that I like them better in November and December, when he is full of guile and has got his full strength. A driven partridge is truly no easy kill. Still, it was good to find a gun in the crook of one's arm once again.

As you see I am now down at Hambrook paying a visit to the Francklyns. Aunt Helen is as well as can be expected, and has been for several long walks with me. What a wonderful woman she is! Consider the frightful curse that has settled upon her. Thinking of her life, one is filled with such intense pity. Poor Aunt Helen. She feels she can never visit her friends because of her affliction. I know it well, though she never says so.

But through it all comes strongly the feeling of admiration for her. Her determination to fight it down, the absolute refusal to give way an inch; the real, true fighting spirit, fighting a battle sterner and more terrible than any in France of today.

The other Aunts are well. Aunt Edith – a philosopher – and no mean one – going as strong as ever. This perfect English countryside falls away to the horizon from the window at which I am writing. There can be nothing quite like it in any other place in the world, speaking of generations of cultivation and simple toil. Truly England is one great garden.

I do not know yet what ship I will go to but imagine it will be a destroyer again. I should not care for anything else. However this inactivity cannot last long nor do I want it to, even in this perfect English countryside.[i]

i.   This letter was ripped in six pieces but still kept. Remainder of letter missing.

Lieut. Frederic Hamilton "Peter" Dewdney, RCN (right) with Nelson friend, fellow University of Alberta law graduate, and future brother-in-law Lieut. Leigh M. McBride of the Seaforth Highlander regiment, 1942.

HELEN FRANCKLYN TO BERTHA   JANUARY 20, 1936

Quarry House, Hambrook, Bristol

My dear Bertie,

. . . One seems to have no time since the beginning of the King's illness to think of ordinary things. The papers today tell us that the funeral will be next Tuesday . . . No news from Fritz lately.

Helen Francklyn[i]

i.   Helen Francklyn's mother Margaret Cunard was a sister of Fred's mother Mary Cunard. Unmarried, Helen lived near Bristol, and Peters family members were often guests at her house through the years.

LIEUT. F.H. "PETER" DEWDNEY[i] TO HIS GRANDMOTHER BERTHA   JULY 15, 1942

HMCS *Q-065, c/o Fleet Mail Officer, Halifax, N.S.*

Dearest Old Bertie,

I received a long and most interesting letter from you today 16 days after it was dated. Your writing which is always good seemed better than usual. Have you bought yourself a new pen or have you found a new way of sitting up in bed or is your back[ii] *better so it is less painful to sit up?*
. . . I couldn't quite make out from your letter whether we are fighting the Germans or the Americans . . . . There was a war fought 130 years ago called the War of 1812. I think you think we are still fighting it. You know, there is yet time, even at your age (118)[iii] *for you to stop a moment and consider whether or not you are misunderstanding the Americans, treating the good old USA, the greatest, most powerful country in the world, a little unfairly . . . . I had dinner at the Chateau Frontenac last night and am picnicking in the Plains of Abraham today beside a statue of Wolfe and Montcalm.*[iv] *It's truly beautiful. My one wish is that you were all here.*

As ever,

Old Man

i.   Helen's son, Lieut. Frederic Hamilton 'Peter' Dewdney, RCN, 25, was serving on Fairmile motor launches in anti-sub operations off Canada's east coast. He enlisted and took officer training at Royal Roads Military College after graduating in law from the University of Alberta. He had a keen interest in public affairs and enjoyed debating issues of the day with his grandmother Bertha who had strong opinions on many subjects — including a fervent dislike of the United States.

ii. In about 1935, Bertha fell down the stairs of the Bank House in Nelson and never walked again.

iii. Actually, Bertha had her 80th birthday a month earlier.

iv. He is writing from Quebec City. Like others in his family he was a keen student of Canadian history.

ADMIRALTY TO BERTHA   NOVEMBER 17, 1942

Madam,

In confirmation of the Admiralty's cablegram dispatched today, I am commanded by My Lords Commissioners of the Admiralty to state that they have been informed that your son, Acting Captain Frederic Thornton Peters DSO, DSC, Royal Navy, has been reported as missing, and is presumed to have lost his life on active service on Friday, 13th November, 1942, when the aircraft in which he was travelling from North Africa crashed at Plymouth, South Devon.

My Lords desire me to express to you their deep regret at receiving this intelligence and their profound sympathy in the great loss which you have sustained.

I am, Madam,
Your obedient servant,

H.V. Markham

ADMIRALTY TO BERTHA   JUNE 8, 1943

Honours and Awards Branch

Madam,

With reference to your letter dated 21st November, 1942, asking for the decorations awarded to your son, Captain Frederick Thornton Peters, Royal Navy, I am commanded by My Lords Commissioner of the Admiralty to inform you that the only decorations that are in the Admiralty are those which had not yet been presented to him before the date of his death. These are the Bar to the Distinguished Service Cross, of which the award was published in the Birthday Honours List of 11th July, 1940 for good services in HMS *Thirlmere, the Victoria Cross of which the award was published in the London Gazette Supplement of 18th May, 1943, and the American Distinguished Service Cross awarded by General Eisenhower for the same services.*

I am now to send you these decorations and to express Their Lordships deep regret that your son did not live to receive them.

I am, Madam,
Your obedient Servant,

R. Gleadowe

ROSALIND VARLEY TO BERTHA   OCTOBER 1, 1943

Dear Mrs. Peters,

I have today received a letter written by you to the Secretary of the United Services Club. It was forwarded to me through Captain F.T. Peters' solicitors . . .

Your son nominated me as sole executrix of his will and it is for this reason that the letter was sent to me. He was a very old friend and was in the Britannia *(training ship to R.N.) with my husband and godfather to two of our children, one of whom served under him during the war. While he was in West Africa I used to attend to a good many things for him — sending out shoes etc. At the outbreak of this war Fritz nominated me — at the Admiralty — as his "next of kin"; he did not think it suitable that his cousin, Miss Franklin,[i] should be so nominated, but asked me to write to her and let her know about bad news, saying that she would inform anyone concerned in Canada.*

Your son gave me his medals to take care of at the beginning of the war, but expressed no wish concerning them should anything happen to him (as was the case with all his other possessions). I feel that these — the medals — should go to the family. I should be glad to know whether or not you agree with me that it would be good not to dispatch them until after the war is over, as there would be considerable risk of them being lost in transit . . .

Rosalind Varley (Mrs. Cromwell Varley)

i.   This is Fred Peters' cousin Helen Francklyn in Bristol, who was 88 in 1942.

Office of the Special Commissioner for
Defence Projects in Northwest Canada

Dear Mrs. Peters:

I was much disturbed to learn from Major Nixon, who was my rep-
resentative when the Distinguished Service Cross of the United States
won by your son was presented to you, that suitable arrangements had not
also been made for the presentation of the Victoria Cross.[i]
Through the Secretary of the Privy Council this has been drawn to the
attention of the Governor General, and the deepest regret has been expressed
by all concerned. May I, as one who has known your family for a long
period, and had the highest admiration for the outstanding gallantry and
accomplishments of your son, again extend my heartfelt sympathy in your
great loss. I am sure you realize that all who knew him appreciate the loss the
country as a whole has sustained.

With kindest regards, yours sincerely,

W.W. Foster

i. The Victoria Cross medal had arrived at the Dewdney house
    in the regular mail, which was a huge disappointment for
    Bertha, as she expected a presentation ceremony commensurate
    for such a great award, especially as the American Distinguished
    Service Cross was presented to her by an honour guard of
    officers and band representing President Roosevelt and
    Gen. Eisenhower.

Dear Mrs. Peters,

This is just a short message of greetings for the New Year and to let
you know that I am thinking of you as the mother of my greatest friend
... The curtain fell on Frederic Thornton's life in tragedy after so much
glory but you can rest assured that everything was done for him that was
possible and I do not think he was less cheerful ... although injured in the
eye. Those who did see him towards the end have my view only — that
his V.C. should have been awarded at once.

Swain Saxton

. . . Commander Varley has not crossed my path this war and indeed it is years since I saw him. FTP, Varley, Powell and I were in his Vengeance together. It was from this ship that our long friendship started. We had a reunion dinner years ago at Romanos on the Strand — Powell by then had left the Navy and had joined a Scottish Regiment. The evening was a bright occasion and FTP in his best form. We had a big table in the Gallery and down below was a table with two men and two charming ladies. Eventually, quite correctly, I established contact and asked if I might dance with one of the ladies. Their escort agreed and she turned out to be the wife of a Chinese customs official. Later FTP, who always thought women rather a nuisance, said he wanted to dance with the lady. I said now for heaven's sake behave yourself, remember she is a lady. His reply was abrupt. I did the introduction and watched. Suddenly there was a break away. FTP came to me and said come on I'm bored with this let's go on. I saw I had promised to dance again so I took the lady back on the floor. "What a most extraordinary and amusing man you introduced me to," she said. "Why, what has he done now?," I said. "Well his first remark was what a nice floor. The second, where are you sleeping tonight!!!", she said. Rather a strange mixture of small talk. However it was typical of FTP to blurt out sensations occasionally, just to watch the effect. However we did go on with the attached party and spent a pleasant evening. In those days we were rather wild animals.

I recall in Singapore we went out for an evening and eventually decided to take some rickshaws and have a race in the small hours . . . . FTP was my passenger; unfortunately I entrusted him with my shambok walking stick. This he tried to Excalibur with and it was only through my agility that he did not succeed in stringing me up. Also I threatened to crash him into other rickshaws, one of which we did succeed in smashing up. By Raffles Hotel we had outdistanced the others and then I had my revenge ripping up his shafts. FT did several somersaults before coming to rest in the dust behind the vehicle.

He picked himself up, and I took charge of my stick. Eventually a Shushi[1] girl passed and of course FT would stop the rickshaw and deliver her in his best memory a sermon on morality!!! We got bored with this and went to get a shore boat. Eventually we arrived at the jetty where he took exception to a Sikh policeman. Delivered a homily. By this time we were in the boat and called to him to get a move on. He still harangued the Sikh walking backwards down the steps . . . . It was then 4 a.m. and the ship was sailing at 5 a.m.. I pushed off so when FT stepped to get in the boat it was not there and he disappeared into the sea. Knowing him I got an oar, and told him I'd knock him out if he tried anything to upset the boat . . . so we were always ragging. I sometimes wonder we were not seriously damaged.

. . . These little episodes may amuse you and make you realize how dear FT was to his friends . . . . My love to you, dear Mrs. Peters.

Swain Saxton

i.   Slang for an Asian prostitute

SAXTON TO BERTHA   JULY 28, 1946[i]

Down Manor, Bromyard

My dear Mrs. Peters,

I have found a signature of Frederic Thornton for you to send to the collector in South Africa, or not as you desire. I also enclose his negative of his snaps for you to have them enlarged as you wish and also an extract of . . . 1914 Navy List.

. . . My love and I hope you will like these relics which are the last I have. I hope you received F.T.P.'s medal as I heard you were having some trouble over that.

S.W. Saxton

i.   This was the day Bertha died at age 84.

Appendix C
Notes on Sources

The Peters Family Papers include reports on the family history put to pen by Bertha's sister Florence Poole in the 1890s and hand-copied by Bertha. These contain stories of war heroes and leaders of renown in the family tree on the Gray/Pennefather side who were an important influence on Fritz as a boy.

Along with the family history notes and more than a hundred letters, several dozen books from the Peters library are held by descendants. Based on their worn condition, many of the histories, novels and poems appear to have been read numerous times in a family of avid readers.

Other sources on Fritz Peters include material in the archives of his native province Prince Edward Island and national archives in Canada, Britain and the United States. Newspaper accounts and recollections of his friends are also invaluable sources. Ironically, the only substantial source regarding his work with Britain's Secret Intelligence Service is the infamous traitor Kim Philby in his memoir, *My Silent War*.

Fritz's ancestors include several Canadians with full entries in the *Dictionary of Canadian Biography*, including steamship tycoon Sir Samuel Cunard, P.E.I. Father of Confederation Col. John Hamilton Gray, Judge James Horsfield Peters, Loyalist Col. Robert Gray and P.E.I. Premier and Attorney General Arthur Peters, brother of Fritz's father Frederick Peters, who to date has not rated inclusion in the publication, perhaps due to splitting his eventful political and business careers between the Maritimes and the Pacific Coast. Much has been written about a prominent British ancestor by marriage, Crimean War hero Gen. Sir John Lysaght

Pennefather (stepfather of Fritz's maternal grandmother Susan Bartley Gray), and a cousin from long ago, Rev. Hugh Peters, who made a name for himself early in colonial America and later as a senior lieutenant of Oliver Cromwell after returning to England. The Peters library includes the 1896 family tree book *A Peters Lineage* by Martha Bockee Flint, now available online.

In addition to family history writings of Florence Gray Poole, an excellent source on the Gray family in Prince Edward Island is *One Woman's Charlottetown*, edited by Evelyn MacLeod, featuring the daily diaries of Bertha's sister Margaret Gray Lord in 1863, 1876 and 1890. In the later year of diaries, Margaret mentions Bertha coming for visits with her "little darlings" — Helen and Fritz, age three and one at the time.

Commander David Joel, RN, got started on a biography of Fritz in the 1950s but stopped when his collaborator Cromwell Varley died. Still, his initial notes of memories of Fritz from 1912 in China up to his drinking spree with Fritz three decades later in Scotland before the Oran mission are an excellent source of information on Fritz from the perspective of a close friend.

Fritz managed to avoid interviews and reporters throughout a wide-ranging life of adventure and accomplishment — until encountering United Press International correspondent Leo Disher, who came with American troops to record the nation's first battle experience in the European Theatre of the Second World War. As Disher, along with Fritz, was one of the few survivors of HMS *Walney* after the Oran action, he was able to write eyewitness accounts of the action in which Fritz won the Victoria Cross and U.S. Distinguished Service Cross, as well as noting Fritz's chats and offhand comments in the wardroom and on the bridge during the two-week voyage to Oran.

The Oran harbour attack and the Allied invasion of North Africa generally are not prominent in literature of the war, partly because the Allies chose to put that chapter behind them when France resumed as an ally against Hitler. The North Africa landings tend to be overshadowed in historical writings by the Normandy invasion 19 months later, even though Operation Torch was in many respects riskier, more complex and involved ships travelling much longer distances than Operation Overlord.

British files on Oran were kept secret until 1972, after which there was little interest until three decades later, when *Washington Post* editor Rick Atkinson produced the Pulitzer Prize-winning *An Army at Dawn*. With little biographical information on Fritz Peters — a man of unusual, antiquated values, motivation and eccentricities — available at the time, Atkinson, like the American military planners who argued bitterly with Fritz in the contentious arrangements for the Oran attack, had difficulty figuring him out. They imagined he was some kind of rogue glory-hunter, an accusation hotly contested by his British and Canadian naval colleagues, friends and admirers, and inconsistent with his service record and thoughts expressed in his letters. The *Army at Dawn* web site, www.liberationtrilogy.com has a good interactive map that shows the progress of *Walney* and *Hartland* in Oran Bay as well as links to historic U.S. army documents.

The politics and misunderstandings that plagued the harbour attack are described well in "Death at the Hands of Friends: the Oran Harbor Raid during Operation Torch", in the Winter 2011 issue of the U.S. Army Center of Military History's *Army History* magazine, freely available on the internet.

There is no record of photos or footage of the Oran harbour attack. With Fritz's disdain for publicity, it is not surprising that, as mission commander, he did not make arrangements for such coverage. Visuals in the dark of night would not be much good anyway, considering the camera technology available at the time. While at first blush *The Victor* may seem somewhat frivolous because it was a 'comic' popular in its time with young boys, it is a valuable visual representation of the event. When the Capt. Peters comic came out in 1962, the editor and chief sub editor of *The Victor* had both served in the war, and every service and theatre of war was covered by members of the staff. Towards making the comic as authentic as possible, the writers and illustrators could check with fellow staffers who had vivid memories of the war that ended just 17 years earlier.[1] Through forums and inquiries I have come in contact with a wide range of people with knowledge or insight on aspects of Fritz's life, such as Col. Brooke Thorpe, son of the Australian pilot who tried to save Fritz after the air crash in Plymouth Sound, and Pete Mitchell, who assisted in the recovery of the Sunderland flying boat's propeller in the 1980s. Their assistance is greatly appreciated.

Glossary of terms and acronyms

Admiralty
The authority responsible for command of Britain's Royal Navy. In the Second World War, there was a Board of Admiralty consisting of a mix of admirals and politicians.

Anglophile
A person with entrenched affection for England.

Anglophobe
A person with entrenched dislike for England.

ASDIC
Sound detection system used in Second World War for detecting U-boats below the surface of the sea.

Attorney General
Chief law officer, and guardian of the rule of law in a province or country.

B.C.
The Canadian West Coast province of British Columbia.

Boom
A protective barrier to prevent unauthorized ships from entering a harbour. At Oran, the booms were made from logs, chains and coal barges.

BGen.
Brigadier General (Canadian).

Capt.
Captain.

Centre Task Force/Center Task Force
Joint operation of 35,000 Royal Navy and U.S. Army personnel to capture the major Algerian port of Oran in the Allied invasion of North Africa in November 1942.

Col.
Colonel.

Commodore
Lowest rank of flag officer (below Admirals).

Court martial
Military court proceeding to determine guilt of members of armed forces subject to military law. Also determines punishment.

Cutter
Law enforcement vessels of the U.S. Coast Guard. Technically, ships greater than 65 feet long with a permanently assigned crew and facilities for crew to live aboard.

DSC
(British) Distinguished Service Cross. Third-level award for valour.

DSC (U.S.)
Distinguished Service Cross. Second only to Congressional Medal of Honor. Highest award for bravery that can be awarded to a non-American.

Dogger Bank, Battle of
Battle on January 24, 1915, at Dogger Bank off England's east coast was the first confrontation of the First World War of British and German fleets in the North Sea. The Royal Navy sank the German cruiser *Blücher*, but other Germans warships were able to escape to home waters.

DSO
(British) Distinguished Service Order. Second only to Victoria Cross for valour.

Eastern Task Force
In Operation Torch, 39,000 American and British troops under British Gen. Anderson to capture Algiers.

Enfilade
To rake a line lengthwise from the side, by rifle or shell fire.

Fathers of Confederation
Founders of Canada as a self-governing nation. The Original Fathers of Confederation were men who attended either the Charlottetown Conference of 1864, the Quebec Conference of 1864, or the London Conference of 1866.

First Lord of the Admiralty
(British) cabinet minister responsible for the navy.

First Sea Lord
Professional head of the Royal Navy and the Naval Service.

Flying boat
Military aircraft with pontoons for takeoffs and landings on water. Mostly used in Second World War for combating U-boats.

Gen.
General.

H-hour
The time of the first beach landings in the Allied invasion of North Africa. For the Centre Task Force, it was shortly after 1:00 a.m. on November 8, 1942.

HMS
His (Her) Majesty's Ship.

Jetty
A manmade structure to enhance a harbour.

Lieut.
Lieutenant (British).

Lt.
Lieutenant (Canadian).

Loyalist
Residents of Colonial America who stayed loyal to Britain during the American Revolutionary War. Following the war, approximately 34,000 evicted Loyalists moved to Nova Scotia (which included New Brunswick at

the time), 2,000 to Prince Edward Island, and 10,000 to what later became southern Ontario and Quebec.

Lt.-Cdr.
Lieutenant-Commander (British). A senior lieutenant in command of a small vessel.

Maritimes/Maritime provinces
Canada's east coast provinces of Nova Scotia, New Brunswick and Prince Edward Island. These provinces and Newfoundland and Labrador are Canada's Atlantic Provinces.

Mers-el-Kebir
French naval base on west side of Oran Bay destroyed July 3, 1940, by Royal Navy gunnery to prevent warships moored at the base from falling into the hands of Axis navies.

MID
Mention in Dispatches.

Motor Launch
Small British military vessels normally used for harbour defence, submarine chasing and rescues.

Neuve Chapelle, Battle of
British offensive against the Germans began March 10, 1915, at Neuve Chapelle, France, about 20 miles south of Ypres, Belgium. After initial gains, the offensive was abandoned March 13, 1915.

No Man's Land
In the First World War, the area between the trenches of opposing forces.

Operation Torch
The Allied invasion of North Africa that began with landings in November 1942, and was completed with surrender of German forces in Tunisia in May 1943.

Operation Reservist
Mission of primarily American forces under British command on Nov. 8, 1942 to directly attack and capture Oran harbour for use in the Allied invasion of North Africa.

Oran
Port city on northwest Algerian coast, 280 miles east of Gibraltar and 220 miles west of Algiers. Second-largest city in Algeria after Algiers.

Original proprietor
Common term for those who received grants of land in Prince Edward Island after British gained control of the island. Based on detailed survey by Samuel Holland, land granted through lottery to military officers and others to whom the British government owed favours.

PAPEI
Public Archives of Prince Edward Island.

P.E.I.
Canadian province of Prince Edward Island. Located between the Gulf of St. Lawrence and Northumberland Strait, P.E.I. is Canada's smallest province.

PFP
Peters Family Papers, in author's possession.

PPCLI
Canadian military unit, Princess Patricia's Canadian Light Infantry.

Q Ship
In the First World War, decoy vessels with weaponry which appeared to be defenceless merchant ships. When a U-boat surfaced to sink the Q ship with artillery, the hidden gunnery was used against it.

RAAF
Royal Australian Air Force. Manned flying boats out of Plymouth Mount Batten base for U-boat patrols and VIP transportation.

Ratings
Enlisted members of the Royal Navy, subordinate to Warrant Officers and Officers.

RCN
Royal Canadian Navy.

RMS
Royal Mail Ship.

RCNR
Royal Canadian Naval Reserve.

RCNVR
Royal Canadian Naval Volunteer Reserve.

RN
Royal Navy of Britain.

RNR
Royal Navy Reserve.

RNVR
Royal Navy Volunteer Reserve.

Sap
Narrow trench, usually made by digging at an angle from an existing trench.

SBS
Special Boat Section. Special forces of the Royal Navy who used small craft such as canoes and folding kayaks for military objectives such as surveillance and sabotage.

SIS
British Secret Intelligence Service.

SOE
(British) Special Operations Executive.

Sten gun
British 9 mm submachine gun widely used in the Second World War.

Texel, Battle off
Naval battle Oct.17, 1914, off coast of Dutch island of Texel. A Royal Navy squadron of a cruiser and four destroyers encountered and sank four German torpedo boats placing mines in shipping lanes.

Tobermory
Royal Navy training base on Mull island off the west coast of Scotland.

Tracer
Phosphorescent bullet which glows in flight, as an aid for aiming.

Trafalgar, Battle of
Naval battle Oct. 21, 1805, off southwest coast of Spain. Admiral Horatio Nelson's massive defeat of the French and Spanish fleets established Britain as the world's leading naval power for a century, and enabled worldwide expansion of the British Empire.

Wardroom
Mess (dining area) and lounge for officers on a warship.

Weihaiwei
Territory on northeast China coast leased to Britain between 1898 and 1930. Along with Hong Kong, was one of two major Far East ports of the Royal Navy. Commonly referred to as the China Station.

Western Task Force
Thirty-three thousand American forces under Gen. Patton to capture Casablanca, Morocco, in Operation Torch.

VC
Victoria Cross

Ypres Salient
Triangular area around the town of Ypres in Belgium that was the scene of some of the heaviest fighting of the First World War. Its shape made the salient vulnerable to German bombardment from three sides, but the territory was steadfastly defended because of its symbolic value as the only part of Belgium held by the Allies.

Ypres, Second Battle of
Began April 22, 1915, north of Ypres, Belgium, when Germans released poison gas against French Colonial forces, whose abandonment of their trenches created a four-mile-wide gap in the Allied line. Canadian forces on the right flank rushed to prevent a German advance, suffering 6,000 casualties over the next two days. Battle concluded with significant German gains but no major breakthrough on May 25, 1915.

Zeebrugge
Village on east coast of Belgium. Site of famous Zeebrugge Raid of April 23, 1918, when British forces acted to prevent German U-boats moored in the port from being able to return to sea. Though the port was only blocked for a few days, British propaganda celebrated the mission as a major victory.

Chapter Notes

Introduction
1. Blatherwick, "Who is the Bravest?", 2.
2. "Londoners Diary — Peters VC", *London Evening Standard*, May 19, 1943, 2.
3. Joel, "Memoirs", 1.
4. Parrish and Russell, with Disher and Ault, *Springboard to Berlin*, 93.
5. Joel, "Memoirs", 4.

Chapter One
Great Expectations
1. Florence Poole, "Notes on the Gray Ancestors", family history notes for her grandchildren, 1890s, PFP.
2. Bumsted, "Robert Gray", 297.
3. Macleod, *One Woman's Charlottetown*, 5, 196.
4. Langley, *Steam Lion*, 133.
5. Helen Dewdney, conversation with author, c. 1970.
6. *Canadian Parliamentary Guide*, 1894.
7. Canadian Bar Association, *Report of proceedings of preliminary conference*, Sept. 15 – 16, 1896. http://www.archive.org/details/ reportproceedin13assogoog
8. Robb, "Arthur Peters", 834.
9. James Nesbitt, "Old Homes and Families: Lawyer Peters Helped Defeat Martin Gov't", *Victoria Colonist*, Nov. 28, 1954, 11.
10. Ibid., 11.

11. "Fred Peters, K.C. Passes but His Work Remains as Witness to His Worth", *Prince Rupert News,* July 30, 1919, 1.

Chapter Two
Growing Up on Two Canadian Coasts
1. Peters family collection includes these books.
2. Helen Dewdney, conversation with author, c. 1970.
3. Col. James Peters obituary, *Victoria Colonist,* May 8, 1927, 1.
4. Bolton listed in Bedford School application as FTP's previous schoolmaster; from e-mail correspondence of Bedford schools with author, 2009.
5. Barman, *Growing up British,* 73, and; St. Michael's University School, SMUS history, http://www.smus.ca/about/history
6. E-mail, author and successors to Bedford School and Bedford School for Girls, 2009.
7. *Cordwalles Chronicle* 1901–1903, e-mailed to author by St. Piran's School history volunteers.

Chapter Three
1905 Going to Sea in King Edward's Navy
1. F.T. Peters, biographical notes written by his mother in May 1943 in response to newspaper inquiries, PFP.
2. F.T. Peters letter to father, March 16, 1916, in Chap. 5, 31-34.
3. Saxton letter to Bertha, June 6, 1943, in Chap. 15, 120-22
4. Joel, "Memoirs", 3.
5. Ibid., 3.
6. Saxton letter to Bertha, March 25, 1946, in Appendix B, 169-70
7. Shawcross, *Queen Elizabeth,* 34.
8. Joel, "Memoirs", 2.

Chapter Four
1914 – 1915 Braving Damaged Boilers in the Battle of Dogger Bank
1. Ted's father Walter Dewdney served in the British Army for 12 years, earning an India Mutiny Medal. He joined the 17th Lancers in late 1854 when there were vacancies in the regiment due to casualties in the Charge of the Light Brigade at Balaclava.
2. Holt and Holt, *My Boy Jack?.*
3. Display at Okanagan Military Museum, Kelowna, B.C.
4. "The German Hospital Ship Ophelia, Allegations of scouting, Claim by the crown", *Times of London,* May 4, 1915, 1, PFP.
5. Citation for DSO, British National Archives.
6. F.T. Peters, biographical notes written by his mother in response to newspaper inquiries, 1943, PFP.

7. Nathan Greenfield, *Baptism of Fire*, 17.
8. Ibid., 289.

Chapter Five
1916 Two Brothers and a Close Cousin in Flanders Fields

1. Letter in Margaret Gray Lord's diaries, in PAPEI.
2. Sgt. Major Dawson to Fred Peters, c. August 1916, in Appendix B, 163
3. British National Archives, *Service Record of an Executed Officer: Eric Skeffington Poole*, http://www.nationalarchives.gov.uk/pathways/firstworldwar/people/poole.htm
4. HMS *Christopher*, Wikipedia, http://en.wikipedia.org/wiki/Acasta_class_destroyer
5. "History of the United Kingdom during World War I: Government", Wikipedia, http://en.wikipedia.org/wiki/History_of_the_United_Kingdom_during_World_War_I

Chapter Six
1917 – 1918 Hunting U-boats and Rescuing Stricken Sailors

1. Deighton, *Blood, Tears and Folly*, 130 – 131.
2. Snelling, *The Naval VCs*, 134.
3. Macleod, *One Woman's Charlottetown*, 188.
4. *Prince Rupert News*, February 28, 1918.

Chapter Seven
1918 – 1939 Quest for Livelihood and Adventure between Wars

1. Langley, *Steam Lion*, 116.
2. Letter from John Bayfield of White Rock, B.C. to the author, July 4, 2010, and; *Prince Rupert News*, July 30, 1919, 1.
3. *Prince Rupert News*, July 30, 1919, 1.
4. Gilbert, "Acuapem History", re S.W. Saxton in Gold Coast Political Service, http://www.jstor.org.
5. "Londoners Diary", *London Evening Standard*, May 19, 1943, PFP.
6. Ibid., 3.
7. Joel, "Memoirs", 3.
8. Peter Dewdney family history notes, 1994, and Dee Dee McBride oral storytelling, 1965 – 2000.

Chapter Eight
1939 – 1940 Attacking Subs from Trawlers

1. Royal Navy service file, F.T. Peters, purchased from National Archives.
2. Joel, "Memoirs", 3.
3. "Londoners Diary", *London Evening Standard*, 5.

Chapter Nine
1940 – 1941 Commanding a School for Spies
1. West, *MI6*, 62.
2. Philby, *My Silent War*, 29.
3. Ibid., 33.

Chapter Ten
August – October 1942 Smack in the Middle of U.S.-British Hostility
1. Churchill, *The Grand Alliance*, 607.
2. Atkinson, *An Army at Dawn*, 18.
3. Potter, *Sea Power*, 570.
4. Letter: Eisenhower to Marshall, Sept. 23, 1942, in *Dear General*, 43.
5. Atkinson, *An Army at Dawn*, 273.
6. Eisenhower, *Crusade in Europe*, 130.
7. Reardon, "Death at the Hands of Friends", 17.
8. Ibid., 17.
9. Letter: Eisenhower to Marshall, Oct. 29, 1942, in *Dear General*, 52.

Chapter Eleven
October 1942 Leaving Scotland for a 'Party' in Algeria
1. Reardon, "Death at the Hands of Friends", 17.
2. Dalrymple-Hamilton letter to Bertha, Feb. 22, 1943, Chap. 15, 117.
3. Joel, "Memoirs", 3.
4. Disher, *Springboard to Berlin*, 93.
5. Ibid., 93
6. Ibid., 102.

Chapter Twelve
November 6, 1942 Troublesome Rendezvous in Gibraltar
1. Disher, 106.
2. Atkinson, 71.
3. Disher, "Oran Overture", 58.

Chapter Thirteen
November 8, 1942 An Enterprise of Desperate Hazards
1. Disher, *Springboard to Berlin*, 110.
2. Atkinson, *An Army at Dawn*, 72.
3. Disher, "Oran Overture", 118.
4. Reardon, "Death at the Hands of Friends", 21.
5. Ibid., 23.

Chapter Fourteen
Friday the 13th

1. Australia's War: 1939-1945, Bill Moore, http://ww2australia.gov.au/raaf/bill-moore.html
2. E-mail, author and Col. Brooke Thorpe, 2010.
3. Hugh Schmitt, "RAAF Pair Reunited: Memoirs of Air Tragedy", *The Western Australian*, May 30, 1987, 18.
4. Ibid., 18.
5. Eisenhower, Crusade in Europe, 109.
6. "Capt. F.T. Peters, Hero of Oran, and Plane Victim, Believed Brother of Mrs. Dewdney", *Nelson Daily News*, Nov. 17, 1942, 2.

Chapter Fifteen
Aftermath 'Silence is the Best Policy'

1. Report, Cunningham to the Secretary of the Admiralty, Commander in Chief, U.S. Fleet, et al., March 30, 1943, 4.
2. "Eisenhower Report on Operation Torch", May 1943.
3. Atkinson, *An Army at Dawn*, 77.
4. Ibid., 77.
5. Ibid., 400.
6. Ambrose, *The Victors*, 49.
7. Cunningham memo to Admiralty, Dec. 13, 1942, Admiralty records, Kew, ADM 1/11915.
8. Transcript of Woodrooffe BBC broadcast, Dec. 3, 1942, Admiralty records, Kew.
9. Memo to Admiralty from Chairman, Honours and Awards Committee, Jan. 13, 1943, Admiralty records, Kew, H. & A. 1057/42.
10. Reardon, "Death at the Hands of Friends", 24.
11. Soward, *A Formidable Hero*, and; *Nelson Daily News*, February 1946.
12. Snelling, *The Naval VCs*, 248.
13. E-mail, author and Peter Mitchell, who assisted with propeller recovery, May 31, 2011.
14. Schmitt, "RAAF Pair Reunited", 18.

Epilogue
Honour, Selflessness, Courage

1. Reardon, "Death at the Hands of Friends", 23.
2. Morison, *The Two-Ocean War*, 230.
3. Atkinson, *An Army at Dawn*, 70.
4. L.L. Lemnitzer, in letter to P.M. Robinett, June 30, 1949, http://www.liberationtrilogy.com/armyatdawn/document04.htm
5. Colville, *The Churchillians*, 138.
6. Churchill, *The Hinge of Fate*, 615-16.

Appendix A
Ancestry of Frederic Thornton Peters

1. Flint, *A Peters Lineage*, 5 – 9.
2. James White Peters, *History of That Branch of the Family*, PFP, 1 – 3.
3. Flint, *A Peters Lineage*, 44.
4. Robertson, "James Horsfield Peters", http://www.biographi. ca/009004-119.01-e.php?&id_nbr=6365
5. Langley, *Steam Lion*, 1 – 16.
6. Ibid., 97.
7. Ibid., 133.
8. "Fred Peters K.C. Passes But His Work Remains as Witness to His Worth", *Prince Rupert News*, July 30, 1919, 1.
9. Flint, *A Peters Lineage*, 30 – 35.
10. Ruth McKenzie, "Henry Wolsey Bayfield", *Dictionary of Canadian Biography*, Vol. XI.
11. *Daily Colonist*, Nov. 11, 1887, 1 – 2.
12. *A Short Account of His Life, by Col. Robert Gray*, Notes on the Gray Ancestors, PFP, 3, March 2012, http://thebravestcanadian. wordpress.com/
13. Ibid., 3.
14. Virginia Gazette, Alexander Purdy, Printer, December 29, 1775, 1, http://research.history.org/DigitalLibrary/VirginiaGazette/ VGImagePopup.cfm?ID=5181&Res=HI&CFID=14417811&CFTO KEN=71617728
15. Florence Poole, "Notes on the Gray Ancestors", 1.
16. Ibid., 2.
17. Weale, "John Hamilton Gray", 369.
18. Poole, "Notes on the Gray Ancestors", 2.
19. Hamley, *War in the Crimea*, in *British National Dictionary of Biography*, Vol. XV, 771.
20. Lawson, Colonel John Hamilton Gray, 5.
21. Poole, "Notes on the Gray Ancestors", 3.
22. Ibid., 2.
23. Waite, *The Life and Times of Confederation*, 78
24. George Brown, "The Charlottetown Conference 1864", The History Project, http://www.canadahistory.com/sections/documents/ federal/charlottetown1864.htm
25. *Charlottetown Guardian*, c. 1938, and; Macleod, *One Woman's Charlottetown*, 189.
26. Stoffman, "The Children of Confederation", 19.
27. Macleod, *One Woman's Charlottetown*, 59.

Appendix C

Notes on Sources

1. E-mail, to author Nov. 18, 2011 from Bill McLoughlin, Syndication Department, D.C. Thomsen & Co., Albert Square, Dundee, Scotland.

BIBLIOGRAPHY

Ambrose, Stephen, *The Victors: Eisenhower and his Boys, The Men of World War Two*. New York: Simon and Shuster, 1999.

Anderson, Charles R., "Algeria — French Morocco: 8 Nov. 1942 – 11 Nov. 1942". Centre of Military History. http://www.history.army.mil/brochures/algeria/algeria.htm

Atkinson, Rick. *An Army at Dawn: The War in North Africa, 1942-1943*. New York: Henry Holt and Company, 2002.

Australia's War 1939 – 1945. "Coastal Command: Bill Moore". http://ww2australia.gov.au/raaf/bill-moore.html

Baff, Kevin C. *"Maritime is Number Ten": A history of No. 10 Squadron RAAF: the Sunderland era, 1939 – 1945*. Adelaide: Griffin Press Limited, 1983.

Barman, Jean. *Growing Up British in British Columbia: Boys in Private School*. Vancouver: UBC Press, 1984.

Bercuson, D.J., and H. Herwig. *One Christmas in Washington: The Secret Meeting Between Roosevelt and Churchill That Changed the World*. New York: Overlook Press, 2005.

Berton, Pierre. *Marching as to War: Canada's Turbulent Years 1899 – 1953*. Toronto: Doubleday Canada, 2001.

Blakeley, Phyllis R. "Sir Samuel Cunard". *Dictionary of Canadian Biography*, Vol. IX. University of Toronto/Université Laval, 2000.

Blatherwick, F.J., "Who is the Bravest?" Military Collectors Club of Canada, 1990 Convention. Public Archives of Prince Edward Island.

Bliss, Michael. *Right Honourable Men: the Descent of Politics from Macdonald to Mulroney*. Toronto, Harper Collins, 1994.

Boileau, John. *Halifax and the Royal Canadian Navy*. Halifax: Nimbus Publishing, 2010.

Buchanan, A. Russell. *The United States and World War II*. New York: Harper and Row, 1964.

Bumsted, J.M. "Robert Gray". *Dictionary of Canadian Biography*, Vol. VI. University of Toronto/Université Laval, 2000.

Burt, Mary E. *Poems That Every Child Should Know: A Selection of the Best Poems of All Time for Young People*. New York: Grosset and Dunlap Publishers, 1904.

Callbeck, Lorne. *The Cradle of Confederation*. Fredericton, NB: Unipress, 1964.

Cervantes Saavedra, Miguel de. *Don Quixote*. Translated by Edith Grossman. New York: HarperCollins, 2003.

CFB Esquimalt Naval and Military Museum. "Commander Rowland Bourke, VC, DSO". Articles & Projects, Local Heroes. http://navalandmilitarymuseum.org/resource_pages/heroes/bourke.html

Churchill, Winston. *The Second World War: The Hinge of Fate*. Houghton Mifflin, 1950.
————. *The Second World War: The Grand Alliance*. Houghton Mifflin, 1950.

Colville, John. *The Churchillians*. London: Weidenfield and Nicolson, 1981.

Cook, Tim. *At the Sharp End: Canadians Fighting the Great War 1914-1918*. Vol. 1. Toronto: Viking Canada, 2007.

Cooke, Owen, and Peter Robertson. "James Peters, Military Photography and the Northwest Campaign, 1885". Canadian Military Journal, Winter 2000.

Crooks, Sylvia. *Homefront & Battlefront: Nelson, B.C. in World War II*. Vancouver: Granville Island Publishing, 2005.

Cunningham, Admiral Andrew Browne. "Cunningham's Report of Proceedings on Operation Torch, 30 March, 1943", 81-82. Accessed July 2, 2011. http://books.google.ca/books?id=MynRmONNSLcC&pg=P A80&lpg=PA80&dq=cunningham+report+of+proceedings+of+operation +torch+1943&source=bl&ots=3Zar2f3GPA&sig=x777yLSjB1c4MZOVD-IZ8lwMLzco&hl=en&sa=X&ei=55JaT8PEKqSkiQLf04i1Cw&sqi=2&ve d=0CB8Q6AEwAA#v=onepage&q=cunningham%20report%20of%20 proceedings%20of%20operation%20torch%201943&f=false

Davis, Kenneth S. *Experience of War: The United States in World War II*. Garden City, NY: Doubleday and Co., 1965.

Deighton, Len. *Blood, Tears and Folly: An Objective Look at World War II*. New York, NY: HarperCollins Publishers, 1993.

Disher, Leo S., "Oran Overture". *Colliers*, Jan. 23, 1943.

Eisenhower, Dwight D. *Crusade in Europe*. Garden City, NY: Doubleday and Co., 1948.

"Eisenhower's Report on Operation Torch". After Action Reports. American Divisions. Accessed August 23, 2011. http://www.american-divisions.com/doc.asp?documentid=138

Flint, Martha Bockée. *A Peters Lineage, Five Generations of the Descendants of Dr. Charles Peters of Hempstead*. New York, 1896.

Gilbert, Michelle V. "The Cimmerian Darkness of Intrigue: Queen Mothers, Christianity and Truth in Akuapem History". *Journal of Religion in Africa*. Vol. XXIII: I, 1993.

Granatstein, J.L. "Dieppe: A Colossal Blunder". *The Beaver*, August – September 2009.

Greenfield, Nathan M. *Baptism of Fire: The Second Battle of Ypres and the Forging of Canada, April 1915*. Toronto: Harper Collins, 2007.

Gregson, Harry. *A History of Victoria, 1842 – 1970*. Victoria, BC: Victoria Observer Publishing, 1970.

Hamley, Gen. Sir Edward Bruce. *The War in the Crimea*. London: Seeley and Co., 1891.

Harvey, David. *Monuments to Courage: Victoria Cross Headstones & Memorials*. Eastbourne: Naval and Military Press, 2008.

Hobbs, Joseph P., ed. *Dear General: Eisenhower's Wartime Letters to Marshall*. Baltimore: The Johns Hopkins University Press, 1971 and 1999.

Holt, Major Tonie, and Valmai Holt. *My Boy Jack?: The Search for Kipling's Only Son*. London: Pen and Sword Books, 2001.

Joel, Commander David. Unpublished memoirs, c. 1958. Public Archives of Prince Edward Island.

Kipling, Rudyard. *Departmental Ditties, Barrack-Room Ballads and Other Verses*. Philadelphia: Henry T. Coates & Co, 1900.

Langley, John G. *Steam Lion: a Biography of Samuel Cunard*. Halifax: Nimbus Publishing, 2006.

Large, R.G. *Prince Rupert: A Gateway to Alaska*. Vancouver: Mitchell Press, 1960.

Lawson, Helen A. *Colonel John Hamilton Gray and Inkerman House*. Charlottetown: Island Offset Inc., 1973, 1999.

Lippman, David H. *World War II Plus 55 — Nov. 8, 1942. 1998*. http://www.worldwar2plus55.com/

MacLeod, Evelyn J., ed. *One Woman's Charlottetown: Diaries of Margaret Gray Lord 1863, 1876, 1890*. Edited with notes and additional text. Hull, QC: Canadian Museum of Civilization, 1988.

MacLeod, Donald, "Henry Skeffington Poole," *Dictionary of Canadian Biography*, Vol. XIV (University of Toronto/Université Laval, 2000).

Manchester, William. *The Last Lion: Winston Spencer Churchill: Visions of Glory, 1874 - 1932*. Boston: Little, Brown and Co., 1983.
———. *The Last Lion: Winston Spencer Churchill: Alone: 1932 - 1940* (Boston: Little, Brown and Co., 1988).

McCulloch, Ian. "Bungo and the Byng Boys". *The Beaver*, Dec. 1996 – Jan. 1997.

Mitchell, Pete. "Sunderland Flying boats". *Submerged: Shipwrecks and diving around Devon and the world.* Accessed April 22, 2010. http://www.submerged.co.uk/sunderlandflyingboats.php

Morison, Samuel E. *History of United States Naval Operations in World War Two.* Chicago: University of Illinois Press, 1961, 2002.
————. *The Two-Ocean War: A Short History of the United States Navy in the Second World War.* Boston: Little, Brown and Co., 1963.

Morton, Desmond. *A Military History of Canada.* Edmonton, Hurtig Publishers, 1990.

Murray, Peter. *The Vagabond Fleet: A Chronicle of the North Pacific Sealing Schooner Trade.* Victoria, B.C.: Sono Nis Press, 1988.

Parris, John A., and Ned Russell, Leo Disher and Phil Ault. *Springboard to Berlin.* New York: Thomas Crowell, 1943.

Patton, George S. Jr. *War as I Knew It.* New York: Bantam Books, 1947.

Peters, James White. *History of That Branch of the Family That Migrated to New Brunswick, Ashburn, St. John, Nova Scotia.* C. 1870. Peters Family Papers.

Peters Family Papers. In possession of author. Transcribed 2008.

Philby, Kim. *My Silent War.* New York: Ballantine Books, 1968.

Potter, E.B. *Sea Power: A Naval History.* Edgewater Cliff, NJ: Prentice-Hall, Inc., 1960.

Prince Rupert City & Regional Archives Society. *Prince Rupert: An Illustrated History.* Friesens Printing, 2010.

Putkowski, Julian. "Second Lieutenant Poole". Shot at Dawn. Accessed September 5, 2011. http://www.shotatdawn.info/page16.html

Reardon, Lt. Col. Mark J. "Death at the Hands of Friends: the Oran Harbor Raid during Operation Torch". *Army History*, Winter 2011.

Robertson, Ian Ross. "James Horsfield Peters". *Dictionary of Canadian Biography*, Vol. XII. University of Toronto/Université Laval, 2000.

Robb, Andrew. "Arthur Peters". *Dictionary of Canadian Biography*, Vol. XIII. University of Toronto/Université Laval, 2000.

Shaw, Michael. *Great Scots!: How the Scots Created Canada.* Winnipeg: Heartland Associates, Inc., 2003.

Shawcross, William. *Queen Elizabeth: The Queen Mother.* Toronto: Harper Collins Publishing Ltd., 2009.

Simpson, Michael A. *The Cunningham Papers*, Naval Records Society. Great Britain, 2006. http://books.google.ca/books?id=MynRmONNSLcC&pg= PA23&lpg=PA23&dq=cunningham+papers+michael+simpson+naval+rec ords+society&source=bl&ots=3Zar2f5xSF&sig=-L5JWuoZzOJCrc3fi7Al ujCPOSo&hl=en&sa=X&ei=V5daT5qQDcWdiAKXx-W5Cw&sqi=2 &ved=0CFAQ6AEwBA#v=onepage&q=cunningham%20papers%20 michael%20simpson%20naval%20records%20society&f=false

Snelling, Stephen. *VCs of the First World War: The Naval VCs.* Gloucestershire: Sutton Publishing Limited, 2002.

Soward, Stuart E. *A Formidable Hero: Lt. R.H. Gray, VC, DSC, RCNVR.* Canada: Neptune Development, 2003.

Stoffman, Judy. "The Children of Confederation". *Today Magazine*, August 28, 1982.

Tomblin, Barbara Brooks. *With Utmost Spirit: Allied Naval Operations in the Mediterranean, 1942 - 1945.* Lexington: University Press of Kentucky, 2004.

Veterans Affairs Canada. The Canadian Virtual War Memorial. Records & Collections. http://www.veterans.gc.ca/eng/collections/virtualmem/ Detail/2495305

Virginia Gazette, Dec. 29, 1775. Letter from Robert Gray, dated Norfolk, Nov. 6, 1775, to his friend in Glasgow. In Colonial Williamsburg Virginia Gazette Digital Collection. http://research.history.org/DigitalLibrary/ VirginiaGazette/VGImagePopup.cfm?ID=5181&Res=HI&CFID=14417 811&CFTOKEN=71617728

Waite, P.B. "Sir Charles Hibbert Tupper". *Dictionary of Canadian Biography*, Vol. XV. University of Toronto/Université Laval, 2000.

Weale, David. "John Hamilton Gray". *Dictionary of Canadian Biography*, Vol. X. Toronto, 1972.

Wilkinson, Stephan. "How Resistant? The Facts and Hollywood Fiction about the French Resistance". *Military History*, March 2011.

West, Nigel. *MI6: British Secret Intelligence Service Operations 1909 – 1945*. London: Weidenfield and Weston, 1983.

Index

Photo Credits

Born in Nelson, British Columbia, **Sam McBride** has a Bachelor's degree in English and journalism from the University of Oregon, including studies at the University of California at Berkeley, and a Master of Communication Studies from the University of Calgary. His career includes award-winning work as a writer and communications manager in the private and public sectors in B.C., Alberta and the Yukon. He is a member of the Association of Personal Historians, the West Kootenay Family History Society and the Trail Historical Society. He has taught family history research and writing courses, and is genealogist for the Peters, Dewdney, Gray and McBride families.

NEXT WEEK—An epic of courage as Sergeant John Hannah became the youngest V.C. of the last war!

PRINTED AND PUBLISHED IN GREAT BRITAIN BY D. C. THOMSON & CO., LTD., AND JOHN LENG & CO., LTD., 12 FETTER LANE, FLEET STREET, LONDON, E.C.4. REGISTERED FOR TRANSMISSION BY CANADIAN MAGAZINE POST. © D. C THOMSON & CO., LTD., 1962.